CSET

Earth and Planetary Science Exam

SECRETS

Study Guide
Your Key to Exam Success

CSET Test Review for the
California Subject Examinations for Teachers

Dear Future Exam Success Story:

Congratulations on your purchase of our study guide. Our goal in writing our study guide was to cover the content on the test, as well as provide insight into typical test taking mistakes and how to overcome them.

Standardized tests are a key component of being successful, which only increases the importance of doing well in the high-pressure high-stakes environment of test day. How well you do on this test will have a significant impact on your future, and we have the research and practical advice to help you execute on test day.

The product you're reading now is designed to exploit weaknesses in the test itself, and help you avoid the most common errors test takers frequently make.

How to use this study guide

We don't want to waste your time. Our study guide is fast-paced and fluff-free. We suggest going through it a number of times, as repetition is an important part of learning new information and concepts.

First, read through the study guide completely to get a feel for the content and organization. Read the general success strategies first, and then proceed to the content sections. Each tip has been carefully selected for its effectiveness.

Second, read through the study guide again, and take notes in the margins and highlight those sections where you may have a particular weakness.

Finally, bring the manual with you on test day and study it before the exam begins.

Your success is our success

We would be delighted to hear about your success. Send us an email and tell us your story. Thanks for your business and we wish you continued success.

Sincerely,

Mometrix Test Preparation Team

Need more help? Check out our flashcards at:
http://MometrixFlashcards.com/CSET

TABLE OF CONTENTS

Top 20 Test Taking Tips

1. Carefully follow all the test registration procedures
2. Know the test directions, duration, topics, question types, how many questions
3. Setup a flexible study schedule at least 3-4 weeks before test day
4. Study during the time of day you are most alert, relaxed, and stress free
5. Maximize your learning style; visual learner use visual study aids, auditory learner use auditory study aids
6. Focus on your weakest knowledge base
7. Find a study partner to review with and help clarify questions
8. Practice, practice, practice
9. Get a good night's sleep; don't try to cram the night before the test
10. Eat a well balanced meal
11. Know the exact physical location of the testing site; drive the route to the site prior to test day
12. Bring a set of ear plugs; the testing center could be noisy
13. Wear comfortable, loose fitting, layered clothing to the testing center; prepare for it to be either cold or hot during the test
14. Bring at least 2 current forms of ID to the testing center
15. Arrive to the test early; be prepared to wait and be patient
16. Eliminate the obviously wrong answer choices, then guess the first remaining choice
17. Pace yourself; don't rush, but keep working and move on if you get stuck
18. Maintain a positive attitude even if the test is going poorly
19. Keep your first answer unless you are positive it is wrong
20. Check your work, don't make a careless mistake

Introduction to the CSET Series

Why am I required to take this CSET Assessment?

Your state requires you to take this CSET Assessment in order to test the breadth and depth of your knowledge in a specified subject matter. California has adopted the CSET series in order to ensure that you have mastered the subject matter you are planning to teach before they issue your teaching license.

Because the issuance of your license ensures competence in the subject area it is important that you take studying seriously and make sure you study thoroughly and completely.

Two Kinds of CSET Assessments

The CSET Series consist of two different kinds of assessments multiple choice questions and constructed response test.

The multiple choice test consists of questions followed by several answer choices. From these answer choices you select the answer that you think best corresponds with the given question. These questions can survey a wider range because they can ask more questions in a limited time period.

Constructed response questions consist of a given question for which you write an original response. These tests have fewer questions, but the questions require you to demonstrate the depth of you own personal knowledge in the subject area.

Nature of Science

Science

Science is a method of acquiring and obtaining knowledge. It is the process of gaining reliable information about the real world, including the explanation of phenomena. It is the development of a body of knowledge about observable phenomena, using the best capabilities humans have at their disposal. The process of organizing and classifying knowledge, through objective observation and evaluation, is a major goal of science. Science can be considered reliable, but it is not infallible. The limits of human knowledge are constantly growing, often making yesterday's science obsolete and simplistic. Science is thus never fixed; it is always subject to change as new information is gained and synthesized with existing knowledge. Ultimately, science is the sum total of knowledge in any period of time, based on the current abilities of man to understand the world of phenomena, verifiable by observable data.

Basic science and applied science

Basic science and applied science share many attributes but are generally motivated by different influences. Basic science is spurred on by scientific inquiry, the human need to explain the observed physical world. It may have no specific goal, but is man's response to questions that arise from human curiosity and interest. It is usually an attempt to explain the laws of nature by using the scientific method. Applied science has a specific practical goal or application: It is designed to solve a problem. Industry and government are institutions that use applied science regularly. Thus, basic and applied science share many qualities, including scientific inquiry and the scientific method. The goals of each can be very different. It should be pointed out that basic science very often provides results that have uses in applied science.

Although basic science may have no stated goal or target, it provides many benefits to society:
- Basic science contributes greatly to human understanding and culture, enriching society in many ways.
- Basic science has been responsible for major breakthroughs that have great social and economic impact.
- Basic science provides derivative solutions that can be used in applied science. For example, basic science was critical to the development of the space program, from which countless valuable applications have been derived.
- Basic science contributes to education and research across the broad spectrum of society.

Limits of science

There are clear limits on what science can explain. The demand for objectivity both strengthens knowledge we gain from scientific experiments and limits what we can explore. Beyond the realm of scientific inquiry are such questions as "Why does anything exist?" or "What is the meaning of life?" These are subjective questions that do not lend themselves easily to scientific inquiry. These questions, and others like them, come from within, and their conclusions, not validated by science, shape the very fabric of a society. They attempt to give meaning to what may be viewed as chaos. Periodically, science will impact these subjective conclusions with new evidence. For example, the theory of evolution is regarded as blasphemy by many religious fundamentalists. These conflicts may cause great upheavals in society, leaving many to wonder how science and religious belief can be reconciled. Ultimately, observation of the external world must stand as the true test of science.

Scientific inquiry

Scientific inquiry is the impetus and catalyst for all scientific research and experimentation. It grows from questions about the observed world and gives us a template with which to apply the scientific method. Steps in scientific inquiry include the following principles:
1. Determination and scope of the questions to be investigated are the first step. These may range from simple to extremely complex questions to be explored by scientists.
2. The design, strategy, and method of the inquiry are then carefully considered, and a model for the inquiry is constructed.
3. The formulation of theories and models based on the careful observation of objective, unbiased data then follows. This formulation is derived from the scope of the scientific inquiry and the questions to be investigated.
4. Analysis of possible alternative conclusions drawn from the models and results of experimentation follows.
5. Postulating a theory or constructing a scientific statement based on conclusions is the next logical step.
6. Defending the scientific statement against alternative hypotheses is a critical function of scientific inquiry.
7. Defense of the theory or conclusion against critical analysis is the final step in the process.

Scientific method

The steps of the scientific method are as follows:
1. The scientific method begins with, and absolutely depends upon, the observation of objective, unbiased data. Any prejudice or bias in the observed data nullifies its validity. Thus the basic input from the observations must be rigorously screened to ensure objectivity.

- 4 -

2. The development of a theory or hypotheses based on objective data is the next step in the scientific method. These theories or hypotheses pose logical expectations that the experiment may yield.
3. Construction of a rigorous and valid experimental method designed to test the theories is the next phase of the scientific method. This experimental method must be carefully constructed to give objective, unbiased conclusions based on the hypotheses posited.
4. Careful and statistically correct analysis and evaluation of the experimental results make up the next stage.
5. Modification and replication of the experiment must then follow to provide a statistically accurate demonstration of the validity of the hypotheses. Equivalent results must be shown from a number of repetitions of the experiment.

Hypothetico-deductive process

The hypothetico-deductive process states that to have an idea and then formulate a hypothesis are essentially creative processes, driven by eons of human experience. Statements about reality are the logical conclusions of observed experience. Such creative propositions are the basis for scientific inquiry. Empirical evidence must then validate these hypotheses. Creative inspiration and scientific validation are interdependent aspects of scientific inquiry. New observations often are the catalyst for creative new theories. Science thus proceeds through creative thinking and scientific validation. There are criticisms of the hypothetico-deductive process: The problem of deduction points out that the original hypothesis may be proved wrong in the future, thus invalidating all subsequent conclusions. The problem of induction, building a theory from generalizations, is that any generalization may be proved wrong by future objective observations. This hypothetico-deductive process, and its problems, is a fascinating subject to philosophers of science.

Importance of a hypothesis

It is important to form a hypothesis in order to make a tentative explanation that accounts for an unbiased observation. To be scientific, the hypothesis must be testable through experimentation. Careful construction of the experiment provides that predictions derived from the hypothesis are valid. The hypothesis must be formulated in a manner designed to provide a framework for evaluating the results of an experiment. In many scientific experiments, a hypothesis is posited in negative terms because scientists may accept logically plausible ideas until they are proven false. It is more difficult to prove that a hypothesis is true because its validity must be proven in all possible situations under endless variable conditions. Scientists tend to construct hypotheses for testing by creating experiments that might prove them false. If they succeed, the hypothesis must be modified or discarded.

Variables in hypothesis testing

Testing a hypothesis is the key to both scientific inquiry and the scientific method. While testing, all variables of the experiment must be strictly controlled except the one being studied. Variables, by their definition, are the processes subject to change. Examples of this in a typical experiment would be the degree of heat or light. In an experiment there are three types of variables:

- The variable to be tested. Known as the independent variable.
- Dependent variables. These are dynamic conditions that may change because of the independent variable.
- Controlled variables. These are conditions that are held constant so they do not affect the independent variable.

A well-constructed experiment changes one independent variable at a time, observing the effects it may have on dependent variables. Only one independent variable at a time may be manipulated, so the experiment will yield a clear cause and effect result. If more than one independent variable were applied, the experimenter could not be sure which variable caused the result. This would invalidate the conclusions of the experiment.

Prediction

These are the two widely accepted definitions of scientific prediction. In the language of science, prediction is stating in advance the outcome from testing a theory or hypothesis in a controlled experiment. Based on objective observation of data, scientists move from observation of facts to a general explanation, or hypothesis, which must be confirmed by testing through experimentation. Another definition of prediction favored by scientific philosophers is the ability of a hypothesis to lead to deductions of scientific statements that could not be anticipated when the hypothesis was posited. In this sense, prediction means what the scientist can verify from what he or she has deduced from the hypothesis.

Criticisms of the deductive model

The deductive model of the scientific method has the following criticisms:
- The deductive model fails to make logical distinctions among explanations, predictions, and descriptions of things to be explained.
- The deductive model is restrictive: It excludes most scientific examples.
- The deductive model is too inclusive: It admits data that cannot be explained.
- The deductive model requires an account of cause, law, and probability, which are basically unsound.
- The deductive model leaves out the elements of context, judgment, and understanding.

Measuring, organizing, and classifying data

Measuring data is a crucial part of the scientific process. Measurements are most useful if they are quantified—expressed in numbers. Measuring is the process of determining variables such as time, space, and temperature of objects and processes in precise numbers. The metric system is the universal standard of measurement in science. Data must be organized in a practical, useful manner to be valuable. Scientists use graphs, charts, tables, and other organizational tools to make data more useful. Data must then be classified—grouped into organizational schemes for easy access and use. These schemes attempt to organize the maximum amount of useful data in a format that scientists can use. Although these steps may be less glamorous than other areas of science, they are essential.

Verification and confirmation of data

A critical distinction should be made between confirmation and verification of scientific data. Verification establishes once and for all the truth of the statement. Confirmation is the testing of claims to see how true they are. For a claim to be testable, an experiment must be devised to ensure the validity of the results. A claim can only be confirmed when we know the conditions for verification. A claim confirmation is always relative to the testing procedures. Test results must always be objective and observable. Actually, no factual claim can ever be verified because there is always the possibility of new evidence appearing that proves the claim false. A scientific law must also be confirmed by making predictions based on unbiased, observable data.

Scientific laws

Scientific principles must meet a high standard to be classified as laws:
- Scientific laws must be true, not just probable. A highly probable principle may still be proven false.
- Laws are statements of patterns found in nature.
- Laws may have a universal form but be stated conditionally. For example, the statement "All living human beings breathe," may be restated "If a thing is a living human being it must breathe."
- Laws refer to a general, not a particular, class.
- Laws have purely qualitative predicates.
- Laws must have a formal language of expression to be fully understood. Such a language does not exist now.
- Laws may be probabilistic. For example, a law may state "Eight percent of all dogs are terriers."

Major scientific theories

[handwritten, top right: System where axioms can be used to derive theorems]

Some major scientific theories include:

- The once widely accepted received <u>view theory</u> is based on an analysis of theories empirically devised from deductive axiomatic systems. This theory has been widely criticized.

[handwritten left margin: algorithm]

- The model theory states that a model may be constructed to correlate to a real system of relationships, and it can be used to simulate real systems. This allows the model to be manipulated and controlled and be able to predict the dynamics of the real system.
- Mechanistic theories do not attempt to fit phenomena into a set of inferential <u>patterns</u> but focus on the <u>mechanism</u> by which data is produced or realized.

Scientific theories have many different structures that may be applied in various realms of science.

Potential energy and kinetic energy

Potential energy refers to the energy stored in an object. Generally, that stored energy must be changed into another form of energy in order to be used. For example, water molecules in a stream at the top of a waterfall possess potential gravitational energy. A body's potential energy is related to either its position (like the water molecules about to fall) or to its condition (as in the case of chemical energy, which is stored in chemically bonded elements).

Kinetic energy refers to energy related to the motion of objects. When the water molecules at the top of a waterfall begin to drop, their potential energy becomes kinetic energy by virtue of the fact that they are in motion.

Laws of thermodynamics

Thermodynamics is the study of energy transformations that occur in a collection of matter. The first law of thermodynamics states that <u>energy in a closed system</u>, such as the universe, cannot be created or destroyed. The energy level in the universe remains constant, despite infinite transmissions and conversions from one form to another. The second law of thermodynamics deals with the efficiency of energy conversions. It asserts that the potential energy after a chemical reaction is always less than the potential energy before the reaction. Energy becomes less dense over time. Since time cannot move backward, initial energy density can never be reclaimed. During an energy exchange, the potential energy of the initial state becomes kinetic, and some energy becomes unusable to do work; this lost energy is discharged as heat. The release of highly excitable heat energy increases the <u>entropy</u> (disorder) of a closed system such as the universe.

[handwritten: None lost]
[handwritten: More Chaos]

- 8 -

Physical changes of matter

Molecules are neutral particles made up of two or more atoms joined by one or more covalent chemical bonds. <u>A molecule is the smallest particle of a compound that retains the chemical properties of the compound.</u> Molecules are the particles that make up matter and determine its physical characteristics. For example, the physical state of a substance (gas, liquid, or solid) depends upon the movement of the molecules that make up the substance, as well as the distance between them. Kinetic (motion) theory states that heat is actually the movement of molecules. Therefore, increased movement of molecules, or increased heat, causes matter to morph from one physical state to another. The higher a substance's temperature, the more quickly its component molecules will move.

In the solid state of matter, molecules are rather confined. They vibrate but stay in fixed positions. This rigidity creates shape and volume in a substance. With an increase in heat energy to the melting point, the substance's molecules move more quickly and eventually break out of their set locations, melting the solid. In the liquid state, molecules move more freely but are still contained within the liquid. A liquid retains the volume of its solid counterpart but loses a definite shape. Another increase in heat causes more-violent molecular movement; some molecules manage to escape through evaporation. Eventually, the liquid reaches a boiling point, at which time the remaining molecules break out of the liquid form as vapor, or gas. In a gas, molecules move freely and prevent the establishment of any definite shape or volume.

 ## Nucleosynthesis

Nucleosynthesis, or hydrogen burning, is the term for the thermonuclear reactions that take place in stars. In the case of the Sun, these reactions provide life-sustaining energy to the Earth in the form of light and heat. This process initiates production of all the chemical elements from hydrogen, the simplest element, and releases energy during each phase. First, hydrogen atoms are converted to helium atoms through either the proton-to-proton cycle or the carbon-nitrogen-oxygen cycle. In a proton-to-proton reaction, two hydrogen nuclei combine to produce an ordinary helium nucleus (helium-4) and two protons through radioactive decay and fusion. In the carbon cycle, the absorption of four protons by an ordinary carbon nucleus initiates a chain of radioactivity and fusion that results in the formation of the original carbon atom and a normal helium atom. When most of the hydrogen in a star has been burned into helium, the helium atoms fuse with carbon atoms to build up the heavier elements.

Fundamental interactions in nature

The four fundamental interactions identified in nature are gravity, electromagnetism, the strong force, and the weak force. Gravity is carried by the graviton and attracts particles to one another. According to Newton's law of

- 9 -

universal gravitation, this force varies depending on the mass of particular objects as well as the distance between them. Gravity attracts all matter on Earth's surface to the planet's core; it is the force that prevents matter from floating into space. Electromagnetism refers to the effects of the mutually dependent electric and magnetic fields. The electromagnetic field affects the behavior of electrically charged particles (electrons) and therefore affects the interactions between atoms, which give rise to virtually all physical phenomena. The strong force, often referred to as the strong nuclear force, is mediated by the gluon, which is the elementary particle responsible for holding neutrons and protons together inside an atom's nucleus. The weak force, or weak nuclear force, is responsible for the process of beta decay and is associated with radioactivity.

Conservation laws

Conservation laws are basic principles of physics dictating that particular physical properties (including both matter and light) of a system (such as the universe) remain constant despite the system's evolution. Some laws of conservation (such as the conservation of electric charge or momentum) are always applicable, while others (such as conservation of flavor in quantum mechanics) are dubbed approximate because they only hold true under certain conditions. Quantities that are always conserved are called invariants. Invariants provide a measure of stability and consistency in physics, and they are the basis for the solutions provided by physics equations. In a classical system, the principle of energy conservation, considered alongside relativity, suggests conservation of momentum, which leads to Newton's laws.

Classical mechanics

The development of classical mechanics, by scholars including Newton and Galileo, revolutionized the way scientific inquiries are performed by placing vital importance on the validation of mathematical formulas through objective experiments. The concepts of classical mechanics relate to the movement of particles at a superatomic level, describing the motion of everything from large molecules to planets and galaxies. Newton formulated the first law of motion (the law of inertia) based on experiments conducted by Galileo: An object will remain in one state until an external force acts on the object. This formulation provides the basis for identification of the fundamental forces in nature. Newton's second law of motion, the law of dynamics, states that the acceleration of an object equals the net force acting on it divided by its constant mass. Put another way, objects interact by exchanging momentum through force. Newton's third law, the law of reciprocal actions, indicates that for every force, there is an equal and opposite force.

Michelson-Morley experiment

The Michelson-Morley experiment, first performed in 1887, was designed to explore the existence and properties of the hypothesized luminiferous ether, which many

- 10 -

scientists believed was the medium through which light waves and other radiation traveled through space. This experiment involved the use of an interferometer (which split and recombined a visible light wave with mirrors) to detect an ether wind. It was postulated that if the luminiferous ether truly existed, Earth should experience this wind due to the planet's movement through space. In the Michelson-Morley experiment, the interferometer would detect variations in the movement of the two pieces of the light wave if the ether wind was present. However, no such movement was detected. This experiment thus disproved the existence of the luminiferous ether medium. The ramifications of this experiment nullified the conflict between Maxwell's equations (which predicted a universal speed of light) and Newtonian mechanics (which implied the existence of different reference frames), paving the way for Einstein's theories of relativity.

Quantum mechanics

At the atomic and subatomic levels, Newtonian mechanics break down and quantum theory becomes applicable. Thus, quantum mechanics deal with the measurement (quantization) of certain physical properties of subatomic particles including energy, velocity, and position. Linked quantities are pairs of observables such as position and velocity or energy and time of measurement. Heisenberg's uncertainty principle asserts that one cannot identify the values of both quantities in a linked quantity pair with the same accuracy at the same time because the measurement of energy, for example, requires time. After measurement of a system's energy is completed, that energy has had time to change without detection. For another example, to find the position of an electron, one must bounce a probe, such as a photon or another electron, off the original particle. The force of this interaction affects the original particle's velocity. Therefore, quantum mechanics often entails predictions of the probable values of observables. Schrödinger's equation assists in these predictions through provision of a probability wave for particles.

Einstein's special theory of relativity

Einstein developed his special and general theories of relativity through exploration of the observation that Newtonian mechanics cannot explain the behavior of electromagnetic waves, which move at constant velocities. The principle of relativity states that the laws of nature operate the same way in all frames of reference. Observers in motion relative to one another will measure the same physical events at different times and in different spaces. Einstein's special theory of relativity applies the principle of relativity to inertial (constant) reference frames in four-dimensional space-time (which incorporates three-dimensional spatial location and time of occurrence), where the gravitational force is negligible. A main tenet of special relativity is that the speed of light is constant, regardless of the state of motion of the light's source. This theory includes Einstein's famous equation $E = mc^2$, in which E is the energy of a system, m is the system's mass, and c is the speed of light. If $c = 1$, the result is $E = m$. This result is referred to as mass-energy equivalence.

Einstein's general theory of relativity

Einstein's general theory of relativity, in contrast to special relativity, is applicable in all frames of reference, not only those moving at constant velocities. An important implication of the theory of general relativity is a new understanding of gravitation. In this theory, gravity results from the warping of space-time caused by mass (energy). This conception differs from Newtonian gravitation, in which gravity is simply the attractive force between objects. For example, the Earth revolves around the Sun due to the gravitational force that operates between them. In general relativity, the Earth revolves around the Sun because the latter's immensity creates a depression in the space-time surrounding it. The Earth rolls around in this depression. In other words, massive objects affect the geometry of space-time.

Rules of laboratory safety

The following basic rules should be supplemented by standards appropriate to individual laboratories:
- Hazardous areas must be identified and warnings posted regarding risks.
- A hazard containment plan must be in effect and readily available.
- Safe control of airflow must be maintained at all times.
- Safe work practices must be taught to all who work in the lab.
- Proper maintenance of laboratory equipment must be enforced.
- Safe storage of hazardous material must be implemented.
- Procedures for safe disposal of hazardous wastes must be followed at all times.
- An updated emergency procedure manual must be available.
- A complete emergency first aid kit should be accessible at all times.
- Regular education on the basics of lab safety should be implemented.

Uniformitarianism

Uniformitarianism is a basic tenet of the science disciplines. It states that the processes which made the world the way it is today are still in effect. This means that careful observation and analysis of the natural processes occurring right now can provide information about the processes which formed the world as it is now known. Simply put, it says that "the present is the key to the past."

An associated (but perhaps less generally accepted) idea is that of gradualism, which says that the processes which created the world as it is known operated at the same rate that they do now.

The doctrine of uniformitarianism is applicable in all scientific disciplines, from geology to the life sciences to astronomy to physics. In geology, uniformitarianism supplanted the theory of catastrophism, which suggested that earth was formed by isolated, catastrophic events, such as Noah's flood.

Geology

Rock cycle

The rock cycle is the process whereby the materials that make up the Earth transition through the three types of rock: igneous, sedimentary, and metamorphic. Rocks, like all matter, cannot be created or destroyed; rather, they undergo a series of changes and adopt different forms through the functions of the rock cycle. Plate tectonics and the water cycle are the driving forces behind the rock cycle; they force rocks and minerals out of equilibrium and force them to adjust to different external conditions. Viewed in a generalized, cyclical fashion, the rock cycle operates as follows: rocks beneath Earth's surface melt into magma. This magma either erupts through volcanoes or remains inside the Earth. Regardless, the magma cools, forming igneous rocks. On the surface, these rocks experience weathering and erosion, which break them down and distribute the fragments across the surface. These fragments form layers and eventually become sedimentary rocks. Sedimentary rocks are then either transformed to metamorphic rocks (which will become magma inside the Earth) or melted down into magma.

Rock formation

Igneous rocks: Igneous rocks can be formed from sedimentary rocks, metamorphic rocks, or other igneous rocks. Rocks that are pushed under the Earth's surface (usually due to plate subduction) are exposed to high mantle temperatures, which cause the rocks to melt into magma. The magma then rises to the surface through volcanic processes. The lower atmospheric temperature causes the magma to cool, forming grainy, extrusive igneous rocks. The creation of extrusive, or volcanic, rocks is quite rapid. The cooling process can occur so rapidly that crystals do not form; in this case, the result is a glass, such as obsidian. It is also possible for magma to cool down inside the Earth's interior; this type of igneous rock is called intrusive. Intrusive, or plutonic, rocks cool more slowly, resulting in a coarse-grained texture.

Sedimentary rocks: Sedimentary rocks are formed when rocks at the Earth's surface experience weathering and erosion, which break them down and distribute the fragments across the surface. Fragmented material (small pieces of rock, organic debris, and the chemical products of mineral sublimation) is deposited and accumulates in layers, with top layers burying the materials beneath. The pressure exerted by the topmost layers causes the lower layers to compact, creating solid sedimentary rock in a process called lithification.

Metamorphic rocks: Metamorphic rocks are igneous or sedimentary rocks that have "morphed" into another kind of rock. In metamorphism, high temperatures and levels of pressure change preexisting rocks physically and/or chemically, which produces different species of rocks. In the rock cycle, this process generally occurs in materials that have been thrust back into the Earth's mantle by plate subduction. Regional metamorphism refers to a large band of metamorphic activity; this often occurs near areas of high orogenic (mountain-building) activity. Contact metamorphism refers to metamorphism that occurs when "country rock" (that is, rock native to an area) comes into contact with high-heat igneous intrusions (magma).

Plate tectonics rock cycle
The plate tectonics rock cycle expands the concept of the traditional rock cycle to include more specific information about the tectonic processes that propel the rock cycle, as well as an evolutionary component. Earth's materials do not cycle endlessly through the different rock forms; rather, these transitive processes cause, for example, increasing diversification of the rock types found in the crust. Also, the cycling of rock increases the masses of continents by increasing the volume of granite. Thus the tectonic rock cycle is a model of an evolutionary rock cycle. In this model, new oceanic lithosphere is created at divergent plate boundaries. This new crust spreads outward until it reaches a subduction zone, where it is pushed back into the mantle, becomes magma, and is thrust out into the atmosphere. It experiences erosion and becomes sedimentary rock. At convergent continental plate boundaries, this crust is involved in mountain building and the associated metamorphic pressures. It is eroded again, and returns to the lithosphere.

Role of water
Water plays an important role in the rock cycle through its roles in erosion and weathering: it wears down rocks; it contributes to the dissolution of rocks and minerals as acidic soil water; and it carries ions and rock fragments (sediments) to basins where they will be compressed into sedimentary rock. Water also plays a role in the metamorphic processes that occur underwater in newly-formed igneous rock at mid-ocean ridges. The presence of water (and other volatiles) is a vital component in the melting of rocky crust into magma above subduction zones.

Metamorphism

Metamorphism is the process whereby existing sedimentary, igneous, or metamorphic rocks (protoliths) are transformed due to a change in their original physiochemical environment, where they were mineralogically stable. This generally happens alongside sedimentation, orogenesis, or the movement of tectonic plates. Between the Earth's surface and a depth of 20 kilometers, there exists a wide range of temperatures, pressure levels, and chemical activity. Metamorphism is generally an isochemical process, which means that it does not alter the initial chemical composition of a rock. The changes a rock undergoes in metamorphism are usually physical. Neither a metamorphosing rock nor its component minerals are melted during this process—they remain almost exclusively in a solid state. Metamorphism, like the formation of plutonic rock bodies, can be studied only after metamorphic rocks have been exposed by weathering and erosion of the crustal rocks above.

Factors

Heat is a primary factor in metamorphism. When extreme heat is applied to existing rocks, their component minerals are able to recrystallize (which entails a reorganization of the grains or molecules of a mineral, resulting in increased density, as well as the possible expulsion of volatiles such as water and carbon dioxide). High levels of thermal energy may also cause rocks to contort and deform. Pressure is another factor affecting the metamorphism of rocks. Increased pressure can initiate recrystallization through compression. Pressure forces can also lead to spot-melting at individual grain boundaries. Lithostatic, or confining, pressure is created by the load of rocks above a metamorphosing rock. Pore-fluid pressure results from the release of volatiles due to thermal energy. Directed pressure is enforced in a certain direction due to orogenesis: This type of pressure is responsible for foliation, or layering, which entails parallel alignment of mineral particles in a rock, characteristic of metamorphism. Chemical activity affects metamorphism due to the presence of volatiles in pore fluids.

Rock

A rock is a naturally formed inorganic object composed of one or more of the minerals found in the Earth's crust. The term usually refers to hard, compact, coherent materials. While minerals are homogenous substances, rocks are heterogeneous. There are three main types of processes through which rocks are formed: sedimentary, igneous, and metamorphic. In petrogenesis, rocks are classified according to their origin. In petrography, rocks are described and identified based on several physical characteristics. Petrology, the general study of rocks, contributed to the formation of plate tectonics as a coherent theory; it also plays an important role in studies of Earth's interior. Due to the (sometimes numerous) different physical properties of a rock's component materials, petrogenesis is usually a more favorable rock-identification technique than petrography; therefore, the former is more generally practiced and accepted.

Sedimentary rocks

Sediments: Sediments are the materials that make up sedimentary rocks. They are deposited in layers through erosion and fall into four general categories. Solid particles are fragmented by-products of weathering. This type of sediment consists of fragmented rocks produced by mechanical weathering, as well as materials such as sand, gravel, and silt, which are produced in chemical weathering. Solid-particle sediments provide clues as to their source areas. Fine-grained clay minerals are formed in surface areas of low temperatures, such as soil. This type of sediment also has the potential to reveal information about its source. Chemical weathering produces ion and salt by-products that can be deposited as sediments. These materials form minerals when precipitated from a solution due to rapid evaporation. Sediments can also be organic in origin. For example, the shells of organisms may be deposited as sediments.

- 16 -

Conversion into solid rock: The consolidation of sediments into solid rock is called lithification. Deposition of sediments in layers leads to the increase of overburdening pressure on the lower strata. This pressure compresses the particles in a sediment and expels the connate fluids (water and ionic solutions) that occupy pore space in the sediment. This process, called compaction, is followed by cementation. In cementation, precipitated minerals, such as calcite, are deposited as a film atop layers of compacted sediment. The cementing material moves into the pore space previously held by the connate fluids, creating solid rock. After lithification, any further change (physical, chemical, or biological) in the rock's component sediments, other than weathering, is referred to as diagenesis.

Clastic sedimentary rocks: Clastic sedimentary rocks are formed exclusively from fragments of other rocks. These fragments vary greatly in composition; therefore, analysis of the sizes of the particles that make up a clastic rock is used as an identification technique more often than analysis of the rock's composition. The sizes of the particles deposited in sediments are related to the energy of the medium that transports them. Conglomerates are clastic rocks formed from the compaction and cementation of gravels. The component gravel fragments may range from a few millimeters to several meters in diameter. Sandstones are clastic rocks formed from particles with diameters of 0.0625 mm to 2 mm. The identity of the cementing materials determines the strength of the various varieties of sandstone. Clastic rocks formed from silt and clay grains with diameters less than 0.0625 mm are called shale. Almost half of all sedimentary rocks are shale.

Precipitated rocks: Precipitated, or chemical, rocks are sedimentary rocks formed from the by-products of chemical reactions. Evaporites are minerals or rocks created through the evaporation of the liquid in a solution. Ions precipitate from the solution and form crystalline mineral residues. Halite (table salt) is an example of an evaporite mineral. Carbonate rocks are sedimentary rocks made up of carbonate compounds, usually calcite or dolomite. Calcite often forms due to temperature changes in seawater, which causes precipitation. If a carbonate rock contains mostly calcite, it is considered limestone (though limestone is largely organic in origin). If dolomite predominates, the rock is simply called dolomite or dolostone.

Organic rock: An organic, or biogenic, rock is a type of sedimentary rock formed from the remains of plant and animal organisms. The bones and shells of animals contain minerals (such as calcite) that can become cemented together after soft tissues decay, forming fossils that make up organic rocks. This type of rock also contains lithified plant remains. Limestone is the most abundant organic sedimentary rock; it makes up, for example, coral reefs, which are formed of fossils, corals, and algae. Coal is a good example of an organic sedimentary rock formed from cemented plant remains. Plants become so compacted over time, squeezing out volatiles and impurities, that coal, a fossil fuel, consists mainly of organic carbon.

Stratification: Stratification is a feature of sedimentary rocks that distinguishes them from other rock types. Sedimentary rocks are made up of usually horizontal layers of sediment (called strata) of various thickness. Sediment in a particular stratum is usually evenly distributed. However, graded bedding (beds with larger particles at the bottom) is formed when sediment is rapidly expelled into a calm body of water. When a stratum is thicker than 1 centimeter, it is called a bed. Laminae are strata with thicknesses less than 1 centimeter. Stratification occurs due to variations in the volume, mineral composition, or color of sediment in transport; the energy of the transporting medium can also affect this process. Varves are sediments (common in glacier-fed lakes) characterized by the repetition of two layers: a lower layer of coarse silt and an upper layer made up of fine-grained silt and clay, each deposited seasonally. One varve therefore represents one year of a lake's development, not unlike the rings of a tree.

Continental sediment deposition: Sediments, and thus sedimentary rocks, are usually found in the lower areas of a landscape. Floodplains are the flat areas adjacent to rivers over which water flows during flooding. Each flood brings with it a new layer of sediment that is deposited on the floodplain. Alluvial fans form when a rapidly flowing river or stream carrying sediment abruptly reaches a basin. The sediment is quickly dumped and spreads out in the shape of a fan on the basin floor. Sediments are often deposited at the junctions of rivers and large water bodies such as gulfs. Loads of sediment are deposited on top of each other, creating a delta. Wind plays an important role in continental sediment deposition, forming, for example, well-sorted sand dunes. Wind is most effective in sediment deposition in regions with little stabilizing vegetation and plentiful sand.

Zones of marine sediment deposition: The distribution of sediment in oceanic bodies is related to distance from land, water depth, the physical and chemical properties of the water itself, and the local plant and animal life. Tidal activity deposits coarse materials, such as sand and gravel, at the shore zone (the area where waves break against the shore). Sediment from land, such as clay and silts, is usually deposited on the continental shelf, which is much broader than the shore zone. In this area, algae and coral, which excrete carbonate, play active roles in the formation of sedimentary rocks. The continental slope is the downward incline from the continental shelf to the ocean floor. The ocean floor (termed the abyss in discussion of marine deposition zones) is where the finest sediments accumulate.

Color, ripple marks and roundness: The color of sedimentary rocks can be used to distinguish them from other rock types. Sedimentary rocks are generally multicolored by their cementing materials. Red is a common pigment in sedimentary rocks—it indicates the presence of weathered and eroded fragments of oxidized, iron-bearing minerals. Organic rocks, such as coal, usually exhibit gray or black coloration.

- 18 -

Ripple marks are distinguishable in sedimentary rocks that experienced strong wind, water, or gravitational forces during their formation. Roundness is a property of the grains that make up clastic sedimentary rocks.

The roundness of a sediment's grains can provide clues about the distance a sediment was transported before deposition.

Identification: Concretions are solid bodies of near-spherical shape that are sometimes found in sedimentary rock. They are formed when a cementing material forms around a nucleus, such as a shell fragment or a grain of sand. The cement binds all the particles together and enlarges the object like a snowball. The sorting property of sedimentary rocks is defined as the degree of similarity among the particle sizes in a sediment. Sediments are described as having poor, moderate, or good sorting depending on the level of consistency of the sizes of their component particles. When sediment strata are oriented in steep inclines, rather than in nearly uniform horizontal layers, they are said to be cross-bedded. Sand dunes (formed by wind and gravity) often exhibit cross-bedding, as do deltas. Fossils are the remains of organisms that are preserved in sedimentary rock in a process similar to the petrifaction of wood. Remains high in the mineral calcite (such as teeth, bones, and shells) are fossilized more often than soft tissues.

Igneous rocks

Formation: Igneous rocks are formed by the crystallization of minerals due to the cooling of molten rock (called magma or melt). Magma can come from the Earth's mantle; it can also be formed when existing rocks melt because of high temperature and pressure levels in magma chambers (pools surrounded by solid rock). Igneous rocks formed on Earth's surface from cooling magma after a volcano erupts are called volcanic or extrusive rocks. Not all magma is expelled from a magma chamber during a volcano eruption. The magma left behind cools and crystallizes beneath the Earth's surface. The rocks formed from this process are called plutonic or intrusive. The mineral composition of igneous rocks depends on the initial composition of the melt from which they were formed. All magmas contain high levels of oxygen and silica. Igneous rocks make up 95% of the upper crust; however, a thin, widespread layer of sedimentary and metamorphic rocks blankets the abundant igneous rocks.

Categories of magma: Magmas are generated in the area from 100 to 300 kilometers below the Earth's surface. Several different types of rock are present in this area; the following terms can be used to describe the parent rocks that melt to form magmas as well as the magmas themselves. Mafic magmas are those containing high levels of iron, calcium, and magnesium. The parent materials from which mafic magmas are formed are commonly found beneath oceanic and continental crusts. Felsic magmas are rich in potassium, sodium, and silicon. This type of magma forms from parent rocks within the continental crust. Intermediate magmas are those with compositions in transition between the compositions of mafic and felsic magmas. Intermediate magmas form when mafic and felsic parent materials melt at depth at the margins of continents. Ultramafic magmas display large amounts of iron and

- 19 -

magnesium in their composition. Like mafic magma, ultramafic magma originates beneath the crust of oceans and continents.

Creation of magma from parent rocks: The various melting points of the minerals that make up a parent rock affect the composition of the magmas they form. Obviously, the minerals with lower melting points will melt before those with higher melting points as temperatures rise. Sometimes, the heat energy exerted on a rock is limited. This results in partial melting; the resultant magma will contain only the minerals with lower melting points. The melting of parent rocks to create magma is also affected by the presence of volatiles such as water and carbon dioxide. Water, for example, can act as a catalyst in the melting of silicate materials, sometimes reducing the melting point of a mineral by 200 degrees Celsius. Water is thought to increase magma generation in many areas.

Magma crystallization: Magma crystallizes when it is erupted to Earth's surface and exposed to the cooling atmosphere or when it stops moving underneath the surface. The crystallization process is the opposite of melting. Temperatures fall until the movement of mineral particles becomes slow enough for ionic bonds to form and stabilize to create crystals. The minerals with melting points of 1,050 to 950 degrees Celsius (such as olivine and calcic plagioclase) crystallize first. Minerals with intermediate melting points, from 900 to 750 degrees Celsius (such as augite and hornblende), crystallize next, followed by those with the lowest melting points, from 750 to 600 degrees Celsius (such as feldspar and quartz). The order of the minerals that form from magma crystallization is obviously dependent on the initial composition of the magma as well as the ambient temperature.

Magmatic differentiation: Magmatic differentiation refers to the processes by which the composition of magma is altered during cooling and crystallization. Magmatic differentiation may occur due to compositional zonation within a magma chamber. In some magma chambers, the material in the top of the chamber (which erupts first) is cooler and more felsic than that at the bottom of the chamber. Thus, the minerals crystallized from magma expelled at the beginning of an eruption may contain higher levels of feldspar and silicon than those formed from magma erupted at the end of the volcanic event. Crystal fractionation is another type of magmatic differentiation. Crystals formed early in the cooling process are differentiated from the remaining magma when certain ions become concentrated in those crystals, leaving lower levels of those elements in the magma. This process leads to the production of starting and secondary magmas (and thus igneous rocks) that differ in mineral composition. Hybrid magma is produced when magma of the original composition is introduced to the chamber after crystal fractionation has begun.

Texture: Texture is one of the most important distinguishing characteristics of igneous rocks because it gives indications of the speed at which the formative magma cooled and where the crystallization process occurred. Volcanic rocks generally form quickly when magma is exposed to the atmosphere above the surface; they have fine-grained textures. Plutonic rocks, on the other hand, undergo

- 20 -

slow cooling processes that result in coarse-grained textures. Observation of a glassy texture in an igneous rock (such as obsidian) indicates that it cooled so rapidly that the ions in the magma had no time to arrange themselves in a crystalline pattern. A porphyritic texture is common in plutonic rocks formed in small bodies at shallow depths. This texture suggests that the formative magma underwent two stages of cooling, which produced crystals of two different sizes. Large, well-formed crystals begin to solidify in magma in a deep chamber. The magma then moves upward to a shallower location, causing the remaining liquid magma to cool quickly, forming smaller crystals around the large crystals that were formed first.

Felsic igneous rocks: Granite, a common form of felsic igneous rock, is composed mainly of coarse- to fine-grained potassium feldspar and sodic plagioclase and is generally light in color. Quartz is also present in granite; it is the last mineral to crystallize during the cooling process. Granite is often used in the construction of buildings and monuments. Rhyolite is the volcanic complement to plutonic granite. The two rocks exhibit similar constitutions but different textures. Rhyolite is usually fine grained, glassy, or porphyritic. Pumice is a form of rhyolitic volcanic glass. It forms when there is a high concentration of gases in the original magma. Pumice has been described as petrified froth.

Mafic igneous rocks: Gabbro, a common form of mafic igneous rock, is generally coarse grained and dark colored. It is composed of pyroxene and calcic plagioclase crystals with traces of olivine. It contains higher levels of ferromagnesian (internally magnetic) materials than felsic rocks. Basalt is the most common volcanic rock. It is very similar to gabbro in composition; however, its texture is very fine grained or even aphanitic (composed of crystals too small to be seen by the naked eye). Basalt is similar to pumice in that it is formed from magma with a high concentration of gases, which results in vesicles (small holes caused by gas bubbles in cooling magma). Basaltic melts flow more quickly than felsic melts. This causes them to cool from a thin outer layer inward. The associated compaction and stress cause fractures called columnar jointing, which are common in basaltic rocks.

Intermediate rocks
Diorite, an intermediate rock, exhibits textures from fine to coarse grained: It possesses a mineral composition halfway between those of granite and gabbro. Plagioclase feldspar is diorite's main component; it also contains a generous proportion of hornblende. Diorite is normally a somber, gray color. Andesite, a volcanic rock, is a common type of intermediate rock. It is fine grained and exhibits gray or black coloration. Andesite often manifests a porphyritic texture. Its composition is similar to that of diorite. This type of rock is more common on the Earth's surface than rhyolites, but less common than basalts.

Metamorphic rocks
Contact metamorphic rocks: Contact metamorphic rocks are those created by the movements of magma near the margins of plutonic rock bodies such as dikes or

Contact with dike

batholiths. The thermal energy associated with magma initiates recrystallization of the surrounding country rocks. The formation of contact metamorphic rocks (or hornfels) is, therefore, a localized process. The region where contact metamorphism is possible is called an aureole; aureoles vary from a few centimeters to more than 1 meter. Hornfels may consist simply of reoriented mineral grains, or they may be formed from the products of chemical reactions between two or more mineral species.

Hydrothermal metamorphic rocks: Hydrothermal metamorphic rocks are another form of localized metamorphic rocks. Hydrothermal solutions are released due to the movement of magma near batholiths. These solutions (liquid or gas) are rich in water and magmatic ions. Their influence creates chemical reactions with the minerals in the ambient country rock. These reactions include catalyzation of the recrystallization process as well as the addition or removal of chemical elements of certain minerals in the country rocks. Serpentinization, the change in the mineral olivine that produces serpentine rocks, is a common hydrothermal reaction in metamorphosing rocks.

Cataclastic metamorphic rocks: Pressure is the primary factor in the formation of cataclastic metamorphic rocks, which, like hydrothermal and contact rocks, exist locally. In cataclastic metamorphism, the movement of tectonic plates causes stress to build up. This stress (and its associated pressure) has a grinding effect on local rocks. At greater depths, the higher temperatures allow the granulated rocks to recrystallize. The products of these processes are termed cataclastic rocks. The malleability of the metamorphosing rocks affects the way they are shaped by cataclastic metamorphism. Mica, for example, is stretched into parallel layers, while more brittle minerals, such as feldspar, are easily crushed.

Dynamothermal metamorphic rocks: Dynamothermal metamorphic rocks occur regionally, probably near converging plate boundaries. They usually exist in shields, which are large sections (sometimes covering thousands of square kilometers) of crystalline rock exposed by weathering and erosion. These rock bodies generally form near large plutons, such as batholiths and stocks. Mineral composition and texture vary throughout the shield. When taken with the assumption that the parent materials were the same throughout the region, these discrepancies are indicative of variable temperatures, pressures, and levels of chemically active solutions present during the formation of the rock body. The materials that make up the shield exist in a spectrum of gradations from high to low. Generally, an increase in metamorphic level is accompanied by coarsening of mineral grain sizes and banding of certain minerals.

Grades of foliated regional metamorphic rocks: Low-grade metamorphic rocks are dense and fine grained. They are formed by gentle dynamothermal metamorphism processes at low temperatures. This means that the metamorphosed rocks are quite similar in superficial appearance to the parent rocks from which they formed. Slate is a common low-grade rock; it is composed of recrystallized shale. Slate's rock _low = fine, dense grade_ _high-grade big_

cleavage property results from fine foliation bred during low-grade metamorphism. Intermediate-grade metamorphic rocks experience temperatures, pressures, and interference from chemical solutions at levels slightly higher than low-grade rocks. Their component grains are relatively coarse; their folia are regularly spaced. For example, shale and sandstone can metamorphose to schist through intermediate metamorphism. Gneiss is a high-grade metamorphic rock. It exhibits bands of alternately dark- and light-colored minerals. Its grains are nearly the same size as those of granite. High-grade metamorphic rocks often display evidence of plastic deformation as the result of high temperatures present during their formation.

Nonfoliated metamorphic rocks: The processes that form nonfoliated metamorphic rocks are similar to those that form foliated rocks; however, the mineral components of the parent rocks that form nonfoliated rocks do not foliate when exposed to directed pressure. Marble, for example, can be produced by the metamorphosis of calcite limestone. Since this type of marble's parent material is only one mineral, the metamorphosed product will not exhibit banding or foliation. Migmatites are rocks of mixed high-grade metamorphism/plutonic origin. At a particular depth, ambient temperatures inside the Earth rise to 600–800 degrees Celsius—high enough to melt certain minerals. For example, nonferromagnesian minerals in a gneiss specimen (such as feldspars) possess lower melting points than their ferromagnesian counterparts. At a certain temperature, therefore, the former will melt. If the temperature then stabilizes and drops, the finished product would be a rock made up of bands of ferromagnesian metamorphic rocks alternating with granite.

lined up
> 1 type of mineral
no iron, lower mp

Pluton, forceful injection, intrusive contact and apophyses

The term pluton is used to refer to any plutonic rock body. Plutons exist in a wide range of shapes and sizes, determined by the conditions surrounding their formation. Plutons are also called intrusive rocks because they are formed when magma travels underground through cracks in ambient country (host) rocks. Underground magma is highly mobile (laterally and vertically) due at least partially to its lower density as compared to surrounding country rocks. Forceful injection is the process in which magma pushes its way into preexisting rocks. Magma can also melt surrounding rocks to clear itself a path or pry out solid portions of rock, which it then replaces. The term intrusive contact refers to the surface between a country rock and an intruding pluton. Apophyses are offshoots of a magma body that are able to penetrate Earth's surface, creating a volcanic eruption.

Types of plutons
A dike is a plutonic intrusion that is relatively thin in width when compared to its lateral dimensions. Dikes are usually discordant, which means that they cut across existing layers or bodies of rock. They usually form in a near-vertical position when magma moves through existing fractures and then cools. Sills are plutonic formations similar to dikes, except that they tend to be laterally oriented rather than vertically oriented; they are often offshoots of dikes. This means that they are

dike

sill

- 23 -

usually concordant (they run nearly parallel to preexisting layers of rock). A volcanic neck is an intrusive rock formation created when magma solidifies in a channel that once connected an active volcano to a magma chamber. When a volcano is weathered and eroded, the magma beneath crystallizes into igneous rocks. A laccolith is a concordant pluton similar to a sill, but rounded. A batholith is a pluton that covers more than 100 square kilometers; if it is smaller than that, it is called a stock.

(handwritten annotations: "Batholith", "laccolith", "Stock")

Minerals

A mineral is a naturally occurring, inorganic, solid physical substance. Minerals have regular atomic structures (crystallizations) and definite homogenous chemical compositions. Some minerals are elements, but many are chemical compounds. These materials are formed through the cooling and hardening of magma, sublimation of a gas (especially near volcanic vents), precipitation (parsing out of solids from a solution), or through metamorphism. Metamorphism is the process whereby a rock experiences changes in characteristics while remaining in a solid state. This occurs due to the presence of one or more of these agents: heat, stress, pressure, or chemically active fluids. This chemical reaction can produce minerals as by-products. Minerals are identified and classified based on certain physical characteristics; the study of minerals is called mineralogy.

Classification
Color: When light waves act upon minerals, certain wavelengths reflect off of the material into an observer's eye, while others are absorbed by the mineral's component atoms. The reflected light waves establish the mineral's color. An idiochromatic mineral is a substance whose color is indicative of its chemical composition, so color is thus a characteristic that can be used to validly classify minerals. Ions of particular elements, such as copper, iron, and cobalt, are extremely absorptive of certain light wavelengths. These elements are called chromophores. The presence of chromophores in minerals often gives those substances vivid and distinctive coloration. Minerals whose chemical compositions do not contain chromophores possess color properties due to the presence of impurities; this phenomenon is called allochromatism. The impurities are often chromophore mixtures that are not part of the mineral's chemical composition. In these cases, color is not helpful in classifying the mineral.

Luster: Luster in mineralogy and petrography is the relative difference in opacity and translucency of minerals (in other words, luster refers to the quality and quantity of light reflected off of minerals' exterior surfaces). This property depends on the type of atomic bonds present in the mineral and thus demonstrates characteristics about the mineral's structure and texture. Minerals with metallic luster (and therefore metallic atomic bonds) are relatively opaque, which means they reflect many light waves and appear to sparkle. Minerals with nonmetallic luster are those whose surfaces are highly absorptive; they usually exhibit ionic bonding in their atomic structures. Various adjectives are used to describe the

(handwritten annotation: "nonmetallic ionic luster")

- 24 -

qualities of nonmetallic minerals: pearly, resinous, silky, dull, and others. Hematite is an example of a mineral with submetallic luster; this classification falls just short of metallic luster.

Streak: The observation of streak is similar to the observation of color in a mineral—the mineral's color is evaluated after it has been crushed into powder. The term streak comes from the practice of smearing a crushed mineral across a plate in a line. The color of a streak sample results from the random arrangement of the substance's component crystals rather than from the substance's crystalline structure (as in the observation of color). The property of streak is a better basis for classification than color because the presence of impurities in a mineral is relevant only when the material's crystals are organized into a regular structure. In streak, the jumble of crushed crystals negates the possibility of discoloration due to the presence of an impurity. Observation of a mineral's streak can also aid in determination of the mineral's luster quality: Minerals with metallic luster tend to be dark and thick because they do not transmit light, while nonmetallic minerals (which do transmit light) appear light and thin.

[handwritten margin note: more reliable: majority crystal]

Hardness: Hardness in mineral classification refers to the level of a mineral's resistance to scratching. A mineral's hardness provides evidence of the strength of the bonds composing its crystal structure. Hardness is quantified through the use of either the Mohs' scratch test or the diamond indentation method. The Mohs' test is based on a scale populated by ten reference minerals arranged in ascending order from softest (talc) to hardest (diamond). In this system, a mineral that can scratch and be scratched by a particular reference mineral has a hardness number equal to that of the reference mineral. The Mohs' scale is accurate to the half-increment. In the diamond indentation method, the point of a diamond is pressed into the surface of a mineral under a specific load; the indentation left by the diamond is then measured under a microscope. The units of hardness attained from this method of measurement are kilograms per millimeter squared (the weight of the load divided by the surface area of the resultant indentation).

Cleavage: Cleavage refers to the ability of a mineral to split along closely spaced parallel planes called cleavage planes. The presence and identification of these planes in a mineral reveal areas of weak atomic bonds and/or wide lattice spacing in the mineral's atomic organization. In mineral identification, geologists observe the ease with which a mineral cleaves and the characteristics of the cleavage surface. A mineral's cleavage is said to be perfect when it splits easily and exhibits smooth, unblemished cleavage surfaces. Distinct cleavage occurs easily but results in marred, imperfect surfaces. Other classifications of mineral cleavage are good, indistinct, difficult, and so on. The direction of cleavage tends to be parallel to crystal planes with high concentrations of ions. Observation of cleavage thus contributes to identification of the atomic structure of a mineral.

Fracture: Fracture is a characteristic usually exhibited by minerals with imperfect or nonexistent cleavage. The term refers to the breaking or crushing of a mineral's

- 25 -

surface (as opposed to the clear splitting associated with cleavage). There are three types of fracture patterns that can be used in mineral identification. Conchoidal fracture refers to a shell-like pattern of fracture, characterized by a series of concentric rings spreading outward from the point of the break. Irregular fracture is simply a rough, uneven surface. Hackly fracture refers to a line of fracture with sharp, jagged edges. Like the property of cleavage, the property of fracture can be used as an indicator of a mineral's crystalline structure.

Specific gravity: Specific gravity in mineral identification expresses how much more dense a mineral is than water. This property is usually defined as the weight of a specified volume of a mineral divided by the weight of an equal volume of water in its densest state (at 4 degrees Celsius). The density of a mineral can also be measured through the creation of a solution made up of a dense liquid and a miscible (mixable), lower-density liquid. The ratio of the two liquids in the solution is adjusted until a specific mineral is able to achieve suspension in the solution. The weight of a specified volume of the solution is then measured and used to calculate the density of the solution and thus the mineral. The measurement of the density or specific gravity of a mineral is useful in its identification because density is determined by the chemical composition of the mineral (the weight of its component atoms) as well as by the mineral's crystal structure (the spacing of its component atoms).

Tenacity: Tenacity in mineral identification refers to the way a mineral responds to the application of deformative forces such as cutting, bending, or crushing. A mineral exhibits brittle tenacity when it fractures under a forceful blow. A mineral that deforms temporarily due to deformative stresses but reverts to its original state with the removal of pressure possesses elastic tenacity. A flexible mineral will bend rather than break under external stresses but will not return to its original shape. Minerals with malleable tenacities can be reshaped without fracturing (gold, for example, can be flattened into thin sheets). Ductile minerals can be drawn into thin strands without breaking. Rare sectile minerals exist that can be sliced into thin sheets through the use of a sharp instrument but cannot withstand the force of a blow.

Habit: Crystal habit refers to the favored crystal growth pattern of a mineral species. Atomic structure is a defining characteristic of minerals; the observation of habit is thus very important in the process of mineral identification (although crystal formation is rarely perfect). The growth pattern of a mineral crystal is closely related to the environmental conditions under which it forms. Pressure, temperature, and the chemical conditions of precipitation are all factors that influence the shape of a forming crystal. A crystal is said to have an equant habit when its sides are of nearly equal length in all directions. Bladed crystals exhibit long, flat areas that are reminiscent of knife blades. A plumose crystal has a series of feathery scales. Minerals of micaceous habit consist of thin, flat sheets that can be easily flaked or peeled from the larger mineral mass. Prismatic crystals are elongated. Other adjectives used for the description of crystal habit are capillary, fibrous, striated, columnar, and mammillary.

Crystallization

Speed of cooling
Nucleation is the process whereby clusters of atoms in a liquid arrange themselves in a solid configuration. At lower temperatures, these nuclei become stable. When this process occurs slowly (when the rate of growth is greater than the rate of nucleation), large, stable crystals form. When the rate of nucleation is greater than the rate of growth (during rapid cooling), the process results in the formation of many small crystals. Minerals with this crystalline composition are inherently unstable and will aggregate into a large, solid crystal over time. Rapid cooling usually produces anhedral crystals (crystals with internal regularity but without external crystal faces). Slower cooling processes generally result in the formation of euhedral crystals (those with well-formed faces) or subhedral crystals (which exhibit intermediate, rounded outlines).

Types of crystal growth
The ideal type of crystal growth is two-dimensional nucleation. In this process, crystals are formed in separate layers. The crystal faces are built up through accumulation of these layers, as the mineral's atoms arrange themselves in the configuration of highest stability (that with the lowest energy). Two-dimensional nucleation occurs slowly and necessitates high supersaturation. Spiral growth, on the other hand, is a quick process. Also called screw dislocation, spiral growth is the continuous growth of a single layer in the form of a spiral. This type of growth occurs in regions of low saturation. Branching growth is the rapid growth of a crystal in limited directions, resulting in a treelike structure. Heat transfer halts favorable growth and causes growth in an unfavorable direction. This process creates dendrites, formed from a single nucleus and with a single crystallographic orientation.

Modes of crystal aggregation
Crystal aggregates are more common than single crystals. An oriented overgrowth is one form of crystal aggregate. This type of aggregate is formed by parallel deposits of one mineral on the surface of another. The surface atoms of the host mineral exert organizational forces on the atoms of the overgrowing crystal, orienting the latter's nuclei into the same crystal structure as the former's. This process occurs most often between mineral species with dissimilar chemical compositions. Cavernous crystals are formed when atoms rapidly assimilate on the edges of a crystal instead of growing in complete layers across the crystal's face. This growth process produces a crystal with deep depressions in the centers of its faces. A cavernous crystal grows when supersaturation exists at high levels along the edges of a forming crystal. A phantom crystal occurs when impurities are present in the material of a growing crystal. The impurities form along the inner faces of a crystallizing mineral and result in an outline of a crystal within a crystal.

Paleontology

Paleontology is the study of ancient plant and animal life. The bulk of information on this subject is provided by the fossil record, which consists of fossilized plants, animals, tracks, and chemical residues preserved in rock strata. There are three general subdivisions within the field of paleontology. The first, paleozoology, is the study of ancient animal life, including vertebrate and invertebrate specializations, as well as paleoanthropology, the study of fossil hominids. The second is paleobotany, the study of ancient plant life. The third, micropaleontology, is the study of microfossils. This field of scientific inquiry is useful in identifying the evolutionary processes that gave rise to present-day life forms. Paleontology also contributes to an understanding of the ways that environmental and geological factors affected evolution.

Fossils

Fossils are the preserved remains or traces of animals, plants, and other organisms from the remote past. These remains may consist of mineralized parts, of impressions left in sediment, or even of entire carcasses. All known fossils make up the fossil record. Scientists use this record to learn about life on ancient Earth and the evolutionary processes which led to life on Earth as it is today. To glean any valuable information from a fossil, scientists must make an attempt to understand the preservation history of a specimen; they must examine the process by which the specimen became a fossil and the natural forces to which it was subjected after fossilization. While certain elements of an organism such as teeth and bone are fairly durable, soft tissues like eyes and skin decay quickly after death. Therefore, to be preserved, an organism must be buried in sediment soon after its death. Since the majority of sediments are deposited on the sea floor, most fossils are preserved marine animals.

Types

On rare occasions, full carcasses of animals are frozen in permafrost terrain, such as the wooly mammoths discovered in Siberia. This type of fossil provides scientists with a wealth of information about an organism because details such as the organism's soft tissue, blood cells, and hints of digested food remain intact. Similarly, small insects may become trapped in tree resin which later hardens into amber, preserving the entire insect. Small bodies may also be preserved when sedimentary concretions form around them. Durable parts of organisms, such as bones, teeth, and shells, may be fossilized when they are buried by sediment soon after the death of the organism. These fragments experience diagenesis with the sediment around them and are preserved. Permineralization is the process whereby minerals (such as calcium phosphate or silica) intrude the pore space of an organism's skeleton. Mould fossils or typolites are created when the dissolution of carcasses leave an impression in rock. Trace fossils are impressions left in rock by the movement of an organism, such as footprints or subsurface dwellings.

- 28 -

Earth's layers

Chemical layers

The crust is the outermost layer of the Earth. It is located 0–35 kilometers below the surface. Earth's crust is composed mainly of basalt and granite. The crust is less dense, cooler, and more rigid than the planet's internal layers. This layer floats on top of the mantle. Located 35–2,890 kilometers below the Earth's surface, the mantle is separated from the crust by the Mohorovicic discontinuity, or Moho (which occurs at 30–70 kilometers below the continental crust and at 6–8 kilometers beneath the oceanic crust). The mantle is made up of rocks such as peridotite and eclogite; its temperature varies from 100 to 3,500 degrees Celsius. Material in the mantle cycles due to convection. The innermost layer of the Earth is the core, which consists of a liquid outer layer and a solid inner layer. It is located 2,890–6,378 kilometers below the surface. The core is thought to be composed of iron and nickel and is the densest layer of the Earth.

Sublayers

The lithosphere consists of the crust and the uppermost portion of the mantle of the Earth. It is located 0–60 kilometers below the surface. The lithosphere is the cooling layer of the planet's convection cycle and thickens over time. This solid shell is fragmented into pieces called tectonic plates. The oceanic lithosphere is made up of mafic basaltic rocks and is thinner and generally more dense than the continental lithosphere (composed of granite and sedimentary rock); the lithosphere floats atop Earth's mantle. The asthenosphere is the soft, topmost layer of the mantle. It is located 100–700 kilometers below the surface. A combination of heat and pressure keeps the asthenosphere's composite material plastic. The mesosphere is located 900–2,800 kilometers below the surface; it therefore spans from the lower part of the mantle to the mantle-core boundary. The liquid outer core exists at 2,890–5,100 kilometers below surface level, and the solid inner core exists at depths of 5,100–6,378 kilometers.

Plate tectonics

Main concepts

Plate tectonics is a geological theory that was developed to explain the process of continental drift. The theoretical separation of the Earth's lithosphere and asthenosphere is based upon the mechanical properties of the materials in the two respective layers and is distinct from the chemical separation of Earth's crust, mantle, and core. According to the theory of plate tectonics, the Earth's lithosphere is divided into ten major plates: African, Antarctic, Australian, Eurasian, North American, South American, Pacific, Cocos, Nazca, and Indian; it floats atop the asthenosphere. The plates of the lithosphere abut one another at plate boundaries (divergent, convergent, or transform fault), where the formation of topological features of Earth's surface begins.

<u>Theory</u>
This theory of plate tectonics arose from the fusion of continental drift (first proposed in 1915 by Alfred Wegener) and seafloor spreading (first observed by Icelandic fishermen in the 1800s and later refined by Harry Hess and Robert Dietz in the early 1960s) in the late 1960s and early 1970s. Prior to this time, the generally accepted explanation for continental drift was that the continents were floating on the Earth's oceans. The discovery that mountains have "roots" (proved by George Airy in the early 1950s) did not categorically disprove the concept of floating continents; scientists were still uncertain as to where those mountainous roots were attached. It was not until the identification and study of the Mid-Atlantic Ridge and magnetic striping in the 1960s that plate tectonics became accepted as a scientific theory. Its conception was a landmark event in the field of Earth sciences—it provided an explanation for the empirical observations of continental drift and seafloor spreading.

<u>Tectonic plate motion</u>
The two main sources of tectonic plate motion are gravity and friction. The energy driving tectonic plate motion comes from the dissipation of heat from the mantle in the relatively weak asthenosphere. This energy is converted into gravity or friction to incite the motion of plates. Gravity is subdivided by geologists into ridge-push and slab-pull. In the phenomenon of ridge-push, the motion of plates is instigated by the energy that causes low-density material from the mantle to rise at an oceanic ridge. This leads to the situation of certain plates at higher elevations; gravity causes material to slide downhill. In slab-pull, plate motion is thought to be caused by cold, heavy plates at oceanic trenches sinking back into the mantle, providing fuel for future convection. Friction is subdivided into mantle drag and trench suction. Mantle drag suggests that plates move due to the friction between the lithosphere and the asthenosphere. Trench suction involves a downward frictional pull on oceanic plates in subduction zones due to convection currents.

Convergent plate boundaries

A convergent (destructive) plate boundary occurs when adjacent plats move toward one another. The Earth's diameter remains constant over time. Therefore, the formation of new plate material at diverging plate boundaries necessitates the destruction of plate material elsewhere. This process occurs at convergent (destructive) plate boundaries. One plate slips underneath the other at a subduction zone. The results of converging plates vary, depending on the nature of the lithosphere in said plates. When two oceanic plates converge, they form a deep underwater trench. If each of the converging plates at a destructive boundary carries a continent, the light materials of the continental lithosphere enables both plates to float above the subduction area. They crumple and compress, creating a mid-continent mountain range. When a continental plate converges with an oceanic plate, the denser oceanic lithosphere slides beneath the continental lithosphere. The result of such convergence is an oceanic trench on one side and a mountain range on the other.

Divergent plate boundary

A divergent, or constructive, plate boundary exists when two adjacent plates move away from one another. Observation of activity at diverging boundaries provided unquestionable proof of the seafloor-spreading hypothesis. At this type of plate boundary, kinetic energy generated by asthenospheric convection cells cracks the lithosphere and pushes molten magma through the space left by separating tectonic plates. This magma cools and hardens, creating a new piece of the Earth's crust. In the oceanic lithosphere, diverging plate boundaries form a series of rifts known as the oceanic ridge system. The Mid-Atlantic Ridge is a consequence of undersea diverging boundaries. At divergent boundaries on the continental lithosphere, plate movement results in rift valleys, typified by the East African Rift Valley.

Transform plate boundary

A transform (conservative) plate boundary exists when two tectonic plates slide past each other laterally and in opposite directions. Due to the rocky composition of lithospheric plates, this motion causes the plates to grind against each other. Friction causes stress to build when the plates stick; this potential energy is finally released when the built-up pressure exceeds the slipping point of the rocks on the two plates. This sudden release of energy causes earthquakes. This type of plate boundary is also referred to as a strike-slip fault. The San Andreas Fault in California is the most famous example of such a boundary.

Geologic faults

A geologic fault is a fracture in the Earth's surface created by movement of the crust. The majority of faults are found along tectonic plate boundaries; however, smaller faults have been identified at locations far from these boundaries. There are three types of geologic faults, which are named for the original direction of movement along the active fault line. The landforms on either side of a fault are called the footwall and the hanging wall, respectively. In a normal fault, the hanging wall moves downward relative to the footwall. A reverse fault is the opposite of a normal fault: The hanging wall moves upward relative to the footwall. The dip of a reverse fault is usually quite steep; when the dip is less than 45 degrees, the fault is called a thrust fault. In the third type of geologic fault, the strike-slip fault, the dip is virtually nonexistent, and the footwall moves vertically left (sinistral) or right (dextral). A transform plate boundary is a specific instance of a strike-slip fault.

Geologic folding

A geologic fold is a region of curved or deformed stratified rocks. Folding is one process by which Earth's crust is deformed. Rock strata are normally formed horizontally; however, geologists have identified areas where these strata arc upwards or downwards. Anticlines are upfolded areas of rock; downfolds are called

- 31 -

synclines. In anticlines, the rocks are oldest along the axis (a horizontal line drawn through the point of the fold's maximum curvature), and in synclines, the youngest rocks are at the axis. Monoclines, or flextures, are rock structures that slope in one direction only, and often pass into geologic faultlines. The process of folding usually occurs underneath the Earth's surface, but surface erosion eventually exposes these formations. Folding is generally thought to be caused by the horizontal compression of the Earth's surface, which is related to the movement of tectonic plates and fault activity.

Orogenesis

Orogenesis refers to mountain-building processes, specifically as they relate to the movement of tectonic plates. An individual orogeny can take millions of years. Generally, mountains are created when compressional forces push surface rock upward, resulting in a landform that is higher than the land around it. There are four broad categories of mountains (which are not mutually exclusive); these categories are based on the mountain's formative origin. Folded mountains, formed from the long-term deformation and metamorphosis of sedimentary and igneous rocks, usually occur in chains. This type of mountain often forms at convergent plate boundaries. Fault-block mountains occur at normal or reverse faults with high dips. Portions of Earth's crust are vertically displaced along the faults. Oceanic ridges are formed at divergent boundaries beneath the ocean. When plates move apart, material from the mantle rises up and creates long mountain chains. Volcanic mountains form from the accumulation of products of volcanic eruptions, such as ash and lava. They often occur singularly, unlike other mountain types that usually exist in chains.

Continental drift

Continental drift is a theory that explains the separation and movement of the continents based on shifts in a plastic layer of Earth's interior caused by the planet's rotation (seafloor spreading). Continental drift is part of the larger theory of plate tectonics. In the early twentieth century, many scientists and scholars noted that the edges of certain continents seemed to look like connecting pieces of a puzzle. Due to this observation, as well as the fact that similar geologic features, fossils, fauna, and flora existed on the Atlantic coasts of continents like South America and Africa, these observers theorized the previous existence of a supercontinent (referred to as Pangaea), in which all of the discrete continents identifiable today were joined together.

Continental crust

The continental crust (sial) is 10–50 kilometers thick. It is more complex and locally variable than the oceanic crust. There is a correlation between the thickness of the sial and the age of the last orogenic (mountain-forming) event recorded at the surface: The thinnest crust occurs in areas of the oldest orogenic activity, and the thickest crust is located near present-day mountain chains. The continental crust consists of two layers separated by a seismic velocity discontinuity located 8–10 kilometers below the surface. The upper layer has an average density of 2,670 kilometers/m³ and is composed mainly of granite. This layer exhibits thermal energy related to the activity of radioactive elements. The lower layer has gabbroic properties and an average density of 3,000 kilometers/m³. The temperature of this layer is thought to be below the melting point of its component rocks and minerals and is extremely variable, depending on the presence of volatiles (elements such as water, carbon dioxide, and sulfur).

Oceanic crust

The oceanic crust (sima) is 5–10 kilometers thick. It is remarkably uniform in composition and thickness and consists of a layer of sediments (fossils of marine life and continental debris) that overlies three distinct layers of igneous rock. The first of these is 1–2.5 kilometers thick and is made up of basaltic lavas. The second, main igneous layer is 5 kilometers thick and is of coarse-grained gabbroic composition. The third layer is very thin (less than half a kilometer thick) and possesses a density of 3,000 kilometers/m³; this layer is made up of basalts. The temperature of the sima is very high along seismically active ridges and lower near oceanic basins. Based on dating of the fossils present in its sediments, scientists estimate that the oceanic crust is only 200 million years old (in comparison, the continental crust is estimated to be several billion years old). The relatively young age of the oceanic crust provides support for theories of the creative/destructive processes of seafloor spreading.

Magnetic striping

Magnetic striping is a manifestation of the magnetic properties of the oceanic lithosphere. In general, the mineral composition of rocks has one of two magnetic orientations: normal polarity, which roughly corresponds with the polarity of the Earth's magnetic north, or reversed polarity, which is basically the opposite of the Earth's magnetic field. Cooled magma, which makes up the basalt of the ocean floor, aligns itself with Earth's current magnetic orientation during the cooling process. While the Earth's magnetic field normally shifts very slowly, it undergoes radical changes, called magnetic reversals, over long periods of time. Diverging plate boundaries on the ocean floor have been forming new crust material for tens of thousands of years, creating new midocean ridges throughout multiple reversals of Earth's magnetic field. Consequently, the ocean floor displays stripes of rocks with opposing polarities. The discovery of magnetic striping in the oceanic crust contributed to widespread acceptance of the seafloor-spreading hypothesis.

Seafloor spreading

Seafloor spreading was originally put forth as an explanation for the existence of midocean ridges such as the Mid-Atlantic Ridge. These ridges were identified as features of a vast undersea mountain system that spans the globe. Seafloor spreading postulates that the ocean floor expands outward from these ridges. The process occurs when the upper mantle layer of the Earth (the asthenosphere), just beneath the planet's crust, is heated through convection. The heat causes the asthenosphere to become more elastic and less dense. This heated material causes the crust to bow outward and eventually separate. The lighter material then flows out through the resultant rift and hardens, forming new oceanic crust. If a rift opens completely into an ocean, the basin will be flooded with seawater and create a new sea. Often, the process results in failed rifts, rifts that stopped opening before complete separation is achieved.

Volcanoes

Volcanic eruption

A volcanic eruption generally entails a build-up of magma (a silicate solution formed of melted rocks) in a magma chamber. Gases present in the magma, such as water vapor, carbon dioxide, and sulfur dioxide, cause increasing pressure in the material. Often, the vent that would enable release of the built-up pressure is blocked by solidified magma. The viscosity of the magma also affects the release of gas pressure—the more viscous the magma, the more pressure will build up. A volcano erupts when the pressure becomes too great to be contained and the gases are suddenly and violently released. The freed gases expand, forcing magma and solid materials upward. The products of a volcanic eruption include ash, lava, and solid igneous rocks.

Eruption types

Volcanic eruptions are classified by their degree of explosivity. Explosive eruptions expel gases, ash, and rocks (such as pumice) to incredible heights; these products affect areas miles away. An explosive eruption can affect atmospheric pressure and increase the electricity of the surrounding air. Eruptions of intermediate explosivity often occur in stratovolcanoes. They are similar to explosive eruptions but their effects are smaller in scale. Quiet eruptions, consistent with shield volcanoes, exhibit virtually no explosivity. Lava flows from the volcano instead of shooting out of it vertically. This type of eruption is often powered by the release of steam rather than the release of magmatic gases. Fissure eruptions are those during which lava flows from a series of small fissures, or fractures, in the Earth's crust instead of from a single volcanic vent. This type of eruption is usually accompanied by flood lava.

Shape categories

All volcanoes are formed from the accumulation of erupted materials into a volcanic cone landform. The majority of volcanoes also exhibit craters, which are depressions at the top of volcanic cones that mark the location of the vent through which eruptive materials are expelled. Stratovolcanoes, or composite cones, are characterized by different kinds of material in their constitution. This type of volcano erupts lava as well as large amounts of pyroclastic material (ash, solid rocks, and so on); all of this material piles up to form a tall, steep volcanic cone.

Shield volcanoes erupt only fluid lava, which flows for long distances prior to solidification. Consequently, shield volcanoes are relatively wide and flat. Cinder cones are small, short-lived volcanoes whose eruptive products are almost exclusively solid materials. These materials pile up and create a volcano-shaped hill.

Activity level

Due to the life spans of volcanoes (from a few months to millions of years), it is difficult to develop a standardized system to classify their activity levels. However, scientists have attempted to create a broad classification system. Generally, a volcano is considered active if it is presently erupting or showing signs of unrest, such as gas emission or seismic activity. Also, volcanoes are usually considered active if they have erupted in historic time. A dormant volcano is one that is not currently active but possesses the potential to become active in the future. A volcano is considered extinct when it is unlikely to erupt ever again. The classification of extinct is usually the most problematic to determine.

Volcanic activity at different plate boundaries

Volcanic activity occurs at divergent plate boundaries most often under the ocean. Divergent plate boundaries are also known as constructive plate boundaries because new crustal material must be formed to fill the void created by the separation of tectonic plates. As oceanic lithospheric plates pull apart, magma rises from beneath to fill the gap; the increased temperature and magma concentration breeds volcanic activity. At convergent, or destructive, plate margins, friction creates the heat energy necessary to melt crustal rocks into magma. Also, the subduction of one plate under another pushes crustal material into the mantle, where temperatures are higher. The presence of volatiles (such as water and carbon dioxide) at subduction zones can force magma out through vents in the Earth's surface. Occasionally, volcanic activity occurs at locations far from any plate boundary. These locations, called hotspots, are thought to exist over particularly active mantle zones which shoot "plumes" of molten material up toward the crust.

Pyroclastic materials

Pyroclastic materials are those expelled from a volcano during eruption separate from the flowing molten rock. They have been found to exist in all types of composition. Clots of lava that cool while they are airborne are called volcanic bombs. Due to the rapid cooling processes they undergo, volcanic bombs usually exhibit aphanitic or glassy textures. Lapilli are small pieces of chilled lava expelled during a volcanic eruption; lapilli tuffs are rocks composed of lapilli. Exploding volcanoes also spew ash into the atmosphere. Rocks composed of volcanic ash are called ash-fall tuffs. Sedimentary processes can act on the layers of volcanic residue surrounding a volcano to form rocks.

Earthquakes

An earthquake is a sudden movement of a portion of the Earth's crust. Strain energy, built up in the lithosphere, is swiftly released in the form of seismic waves which, among other things, cause vibratory ground motion. The majority of these events occur at high-stress tectonic plate boundaries. The rupture zone is the total size of the fault that slips; the larger the rupture zone, the greater the effects of the earthquake. The focus, or hypocenter, of an earthquake is the location from which the seismic waves seem to emanate. The epicenter is the location on the Earth's crust above an earthquake's hypocenter. Earthquakes are classified according to their focus depths: shallow (0-70 kilometers below the surface), intermediate (70-300 kilometers below the surface), or deep (below 300 kilometers deep).

Elastic rebound theory
In periods between seismic events, tectonic plates move relative to one another except at their boundaries, where the rocks are locked together. The differential movement of the plates causes the rocks near the plate boundaries to undergo elastic deformation and build up a level of strain. This process occurs slowly and for long periods of time. When the strain along the fault becomes powerful enough to overcome the strength of the rocks, they snap or rebound into place, aligning themselves in seconds with the plates, which have been moving slowly but steadily for tens or hundreds of years. According to elastic rebound theory, this release of strain energy constitutes an earthquake.

Interplate and intraplate earthquakes
An interplate earthquake occurs at a boundary between two tectonic plates. The slippage of rocks on either side of the boundary results in deformation of the surrounding land and the release of seismic waves. Interplate earthquakes are more common than intraplate earthquakes. Although plate tectonics envisions the Earth's surface as a series of plates moving past one another, we must remember that those plates are fractured aspects of the ancient crust. Intraplate earthquakes occur along highly stressed fault lines on the interior of tectonic plates. Because the faults that cause these earthquakes are often below the surface, they are difficult to predict or study.

Teleseism, deep-focus earthquake, and blind thrust earthquake
A teleseism is measurable movement of a location on the Earth's surface caused by a large earthquake in a distant location. Generally, earthquakes of magnitude 5.3 or higher at any location cause these tremors (discernible through the use of modern seismic-detection equipment) in any part of the world. A deep-focus earthquake originates 600–700 kilometers beneath the Earth's surface. Scientists believe that deep-focus earthquakes are related to catastrophic phase changes in the Earth's interior. A blind thrust earthquake occurs along a previously undetected thrust fault. Blind thrust faults usually form in high-stress zones near large plate boundaries. This type of earthquake can be the most deadly, due to the fact that city

- 36 -

planners cannot take the location of an unknown fault line into consideration during new construction and earthquake preparedness planning.

Foreshocks and aftershocks

A foreshock is a small earthquake that occasionally precedes a larger, principal earthquake. Foreshocks can potentially be used to aid in the prediction of larger, more-dangerous events. They occur less often than aftershocks, which are small tremors following a principal earthquake. According to Omori's law, the rate of aftershocks is proportional to the inverse of the time lapse since the main earthquake. Some aftershocks last longer than others: In the New Madrid Seismic Zone, the effects of huge earthquakes in 1811–1812 are still being felt. Aftershocks have the potential to exponentially increase the damage caused by a large earthquake. For example, an aftershock can level buildings that have already suffered damage during the main event. The unpredictability of aftershocks makes them especially dangerous.

Damage

The following are earthquake-damage–related terms:
- A tsunami is a series of waves created by sudden, large-scale displacement of water in a large body of water. Tsunamis are not tidal waves (though many use the terms interchangeably), but strong, seemingly endless tides originating in the depths of the body of water (rather than on the surface). The height of a tsunami and its energy increase as it nears a shoreline; a powerful tsunami has the strength to flatten a coastline.
- A seiche is a related phenomenon: It is a standing wave generated by a disturbance (usually seismic or wind-related) in a body of water. A seiche moves vertically as gravity attempts to restore horizontal equilibrium on the water's surface. Liquefaction basically refers to the suspension of soil particles in water. Earthquakes increase water pressure, which increases the potential mobility of soil particles. This, in turn, significantly decreases the ability of said soil to support building foundations and upper layers of soil.
- A landslide is an effect of liquefaction in which portions of the Earth's surface are rapidly displaced.

Preparation

Earthquakes cannot be prevented, and techniques that have been suggested to predict earthquakes are unreliable and unproven. Therefore, the best way to prevent property damage and harm to humans during an earthquake is to lessen their effects through engineering. For example, selecting a building site atop a formation of solid rock can lessen earthquake damage because such sites are more stable than unconsolidated or water-laden ground. Obviously, knowledge of fault lines can also aid in the selection of optimal building sites. The type of buildings we construct can also affect the amount of damages endured during an earthquake. For instance, the use of reinforcing rods and construction of buildings that are capable of oscillating as a unit can prevent serious damage to such structures during an earthquake. A suspension bridge is an example of a structure that can flex during earthquakes, lessening its potential to be damaged during a seismic event.

Prediction

Many different theories have been put forth regarding the methodology of earthquake prediction. These ideas have ranged from analysis of the behavior of animals to observation of changes in the electrical conductivity of granite in a quake zone. Hypotheses suggesting that earthquakes can be predicted through, for example, measurement of variations in the gravitational pull of the Sun, planets, and Moon have not been verified. Other theories, such as analysis of the time and space patterns created by past earthquakes in a certain area to predict an upcoming quake, have experienced some validation. An increase in the radon levels in an area, the appearance of strange clouds, foreshocks, and the detection of strain in crustal rocks have all been suggested as possible indicators of a looming earthquake. Ultimately however, there is no method of earthquake prediction that is consistently and reliably accurate.

Seismic waves

Seismic waves are mechanical disturbances that transfer energy. These waves are created by earthquakes or explosions. Body waves travel within the Earth's interior on curved pathways due to the various densities of the Earth's composite materials. The category of body waves is further subdivided into primary (P) waves and secondary (S) waves. P waves can travel through any material (although they move fastest in a solid), alternately compressing and dilating such materials in the direction of wave movement. They are similar to sound waves and move more quickly than S waves. S waves (or transverse waves) can only travel through solids. They displace the ground perpendicularly to the direction of wave movement to one side and then to the other. Surface waves, similar to water waves, travel above the Earth's surface and cause more damage than body waves due to their low frequencies. Rayleigh waves perpetuate ground roll during earthquakes: The Earth's surface ripples like the surface of water. Love waves move marginally more quickly than Rayleigh waves and cause horizontal shearing of the Earth's crust.

The study of seismic waves reveals the magnitude of and distance to a seismic disturbance. Seismology can also provide valuable information about inaccessible parts of the Earth's interior. Seismic waves radiate outward in all directions from such a disturbance, and therefore travel through the depths of the Earth before arrival at distant seismograph stations. Understanding the properties of body waves (for instance, the materials they can travel through and the effects of density, pressure, and temperature upon the velocities at which they can travel through those materials) enables seismologists to make reasonable inferences about the composition of the inner Earth, based upon seismographic data collected from all over the world.

Seismic data and inner earth

Based upon information about the variations in the velocities of primary (P) and secondary (S) waves at different locations on the surface, scientists have created a hypothetical structure of the outermost 700 kilometers of the Earth (which expands accepted theories about the crust, mantle, and core layers). Body waves travel at high velocities through the strong, solid lithosphere. Waves moving through the asthenosphere travel more slowly, suggesting that this layer is 1–10% molten and relatively weak. The presence of the Mohorovicic discontinuity (the crust-mantle boundary) is demonstrated by a sharp increase in the velocity of body waves at a depth of 6–70 kilometers. The mesosphere is the mantle zone beneath the asthenosphere, where increased pressure strengthens the rock again. Extreme increases in wave velocity occur at 350–400 kilometers and at 650–700 kilometers below the surface, suggesting phase transitions at these depths, in which the density of the materials becomes much higher due to increased pressure. At these stages, iron and magnesium are thought to break down (due to extreme pressure) into silicates.

Generally, wave velocities increase steadily from 700–2,900 kilometers below the surface, indicating increasing pressure and the presence of increasingly dense mantle material in the form of iron and magnesium silicates. At 2,900 kilometers, primary (P) wave velocities experience a drastic drop, and secondary (S) waves disappear completely. This data indicates that the rock at 2,900 kilometers changes abruptly from a solid to a liquid state (since S waves cannot travel through liquid and P waves move through liquid very slowly). Thus, 2,900 kilometers below surface level is believed to be the boundary between the mesosphere and the liquid outer core. At a depth of 5,100 kilometers, observed P wave velocities rise sharply once again, and S waves are faintly detectable. This change in body wave velocities provides strong evidence for the presence of a final phase change between the liquid outer core and the inner core, which is thought be solid and composed mainly of iron.

Seismograph

The seismograph, or seismometer, is an instrument used to record the waves released during an earthquake or other seismic event. This instrument, originally constructed by Zhang Heng in 132, has evolved into a sophisticated machine capable of measuring waves of different types, sizes, and directions. Seismologists study and compare these records to shed light on the processes that occur during an earthquake and to discover information about the inner Earth. The seismograph consists of a large mass suspended from a frame, which is secured to the Earth. Gravity holds the massive object in a reference position while seismic waves initiate movement of the Earth's surface and the seismograph's foundation. The instrument then records the relative motion between the suspended object and the frame. Advances in physics and electronics have aided in the process of perfecting the seismograph. Modern instruments are capable of recording and differentiating north-south, east-west, and up-down dimensions of ground movement.

Geomorphology

Geomorphology is a subdiscipline of physical geography. Geomorphologists study the origins and formative processes of landforms. Observation of weathering and erosion processes, the movement of tectonic plates, mass movements, and the effects of human activity on the environment all contribute to an understanding of the formation and evolution of landforms. Aerial photography (from within Earth's atmosphere or from space) can aid geomorphologists in their quests. Photos taken at intervals allow them to study, for example, the creative and destructive events that occur at plate boundaries. Landscape photography also enables geomorphologists to observe long-term processes of stream erosion. Geomorphology can be applied to prediction and prevention of natural hazards such as landslides; it can also be helpful in assessing and rectifying damage to the natural environment by humans.

Weathering

The rocks at Earth's surface experience physical, biological, and chemical processes that are much different from the processes ambient during their formations. The operation of these processes on Earth materials is called weathering.

Mechanical weathering

Mechanical weathering causes disintegration of rocks and minerals. In this process, the affected rocks break apart into small fragments but retain their chemical compositions. This type of weathering occurs due to the presence of joints, or cracks, in rocks that allow the penetration of water and vegetative roots. Mechanical weathering occurs most often in cooler climates. The subtypes of mechanical weathering are pressure release, exfoliation, freeze-thaw, and salt-crystal growth:
- Pressure release, or surface unloading, occurs when erosion removes materials overlying rock. Decreased pressure causes the underlying rocks to expand and fracture.
- Exfoliation often occurs in regions with some moisture that experience substantial diurnal temperature changes. Rocks are subjected to heat during the day, which causes them to expand. At night, the much cooler temperatures cause the rocks to compact. The repeated expansion and contraction creates stress in the outer layers of the rocks, which eventually begin to "peel" off in thin layers. Exfoliation can also be caused by pressure release.
- Freeze-thaw operates when water, which has penetrated the joints of a rock, freezes and expands. The resultant pressure widens the joints and can even shatter the rock. If the rock does not fracture, the thawing of ice in the joints admits water further into the rock. Continuous, long-term freeze-thaw activity weakens rocks.

- In salt-crystal growth, the evaporation of saline solutions within rocks leaves salt crystals behind. Pressures accompanying this crystallization can be very high.

Chemical weathering

Chemical weathering refers to the processes by which rocks experience chemical changes (such as decomposition and decay) due to the influence of organic acids. Chemical weathering occurs most often in high temperature, high humidity climates. The two types of weathering are not mutually exclusive; they often occur side by side. The subtypes of chemical weathering are hydration, hydrolysis, oxidation, and solution:

- Hydration occurs when salt minerals, which are part of a rock, expand and change due to the absorption of water. For example, anhydrite changes to gypsum with the addition of water. Hydration can cause rocks to fragment mechanically.
- Hydrolysis involves a chemical reaction between acidic water and a rock-forming mineral. The interaction breaks the rock down into new materials. For instance, the chemical reaction between feldspar and acidic water produces quartz and clay.
- Oxidation, or rusting, which results in yellow, brown, or red discoloration, occurs in iron-bearing minerals when they are exposed to the atmosphere.
- Solution is the weathering process whereby an organic acid interacts with certain minerals in a rock, producing ions that are then washed away by erosion. Solution, therefore, is a gradual dissolving process. It produces underground channels and caverns.

Erosion

Erosion also occurs simultaneously with weathering. This term refers to the transportation of Earth materials by wind, water, gravity, and sometimes living organisms.

Erosion landform: An erosion landform is a landform created by the processes of weathering and erosion. For example, a cliff is an erosion landform. Cliffs are formed when relatively strong rocks are exposed to centuries of wind and water, weathering and erosion. Sandstone, limestone, and basalt are examples of rocks that commonly become cliffs. The canyon provides the classic instance of an erosion landform. Canyons are formed from many years of weathering and erosion processes (often water-based), usually operating on a plateau (a mountain which has been eroded down to a flat but elevated surface). Strata of rocks that resisted the destructive processes remain visible in the canyon walls.

Effects of human activity

Human activity can affect the resistance of solid materials such as soil to erosion processes. Construction activity has the largest effect on the stability of soil— clearing trees and other vegetation makes portions of land especially susceptible to runoff. Agriculture is another industry that may adversely affect the resistance of Earth materials to erosion. Animal husbandry and urban development can also lead to increases (smaller than other activities, but still significant) in the levels of eroding materials. With increased erosion, Earth materials are more likely to shift through mass movements, changing natural landscapes and placing humans and other organisms in danger. Increased air pollution can catalyze erosive processes by increasing the speed of rock decay.

Mass movement

A mass movement (also called mass wasting) is the downward movement of large amounts of rock and debris due to gravitational forces. The speed at which the material will move and the amount of dislodged material are affected by several factors: the amount of water in the affected material; the climate; the type and extent of weathering; the steepness of the incline; the presence or absence of rooted vegetation; the type of bedrock present and its condition; and the presence or absence of seismic activity. Mass movements cause changes in the landscape of an area. They can also place humans and animals in the affected area in danger.

Rockfall

A rockfall is a mass movement wherein various amounts of rock material fall very rapidly (at speeds of 99 miles per hour or more) from a cliff face. This movement may involve a single rock or boulder or may spur an avalanche of tons of rock. The pile of rocks that results from a rockfall is termed a talus. When it occurs at a mountain base, a talus may prevent weathering of the mountain. A rockfall may be triggered by an earthquake, excessive rain, ice wedging (common on mountains), or human activity. Such a mass movement may, in turn, spawn an avalanche, a rockfall that contributes to a debris flow. The materials in motion in a rockfall often leave "scars" on the slope from which they fall.

Landslide

The term landslide may be used to designate several different downslope movements. Normally, a landslide involves the movement of soil and rock as a more or less coherent mass down a slope, although either the bedrock itself or the soil which overlays it may move independently. There are two main categories of landslides. Glides, or translational slides, which entails a large portion of rock detached from its bedrock which "glides" outward and downward along a slope. A slump (or rotational slide) involves the motion of a relatively cohesive mass along a concave plane—the upper part of the sliding mass ends up below ground level, and the bottom part of the mass ends up above it.

Prediction and prevention: The study of soils in an area is useful in estimating the frequency of geological hazards, and therefore the likelihood of the occurrence of a mass movement in the near future. For instance, poorly developed soil in an area is indicative of a mass movement in the recent past; well-developed soil indicates that an area has been free of such geological events for a period of time.

- 42 -

Also, observation of erosive processes, groundwater drainage, and slope steepness can aid in the prediction of geological hazard occurrence. Civil engineers may attempt to stabilize potential areas of mass movement by several methods. For example, slides may be regraded to lesser inclines. Also, engineers may try to reduce the amount of water in materials on a slope through the implementation of drainage systems or by covering the slope surface with a material, such as plastic, to keep water out. Another method of slope stabilization is the consolidation of loose soil and rock fragments.

Flow

Flow is a type of mass movement that entails viscous motion of surface materials. Flows are characterized by motion of the internal grains of the moving mass (unlike slides). Also, they do not include a clear barrier between the flow material and a stable surface underneath. The velocity of a flow is widely various, dependent on the slope upon which it travels and the presence or absence of water. Flows generally involve one of three types of material: earth, mud, or debris. An earth flow is often initiated at the end of a slump slide, when the block of sliding material breaks apart. A mud flow involves the motions of soil and relatively high proportions of water. Increased water content increases the velocity of the moving mass from that of an earth flow. Mud flows are common in deserts. A debris flow is similar to a mud flow; often, the only distinction between the two is the size of the particles in motion. The motions of both debris flows and mud flows tend to follow pre-existing channels.

Creep

Creep is another landscape-altering mass movement. It involves a shallow mass of soil material moving slowly downward. This type of movement usually occurs so slowly that no one notices it. Creep can be caused by freeze-thaw or wet-dry cycles, depending on the characteristics of the bedrock materials. As with other types of mass movements, the introduction of high amounts of water into creep material will cause it to move more quickly. Though creep does not pose an immediate threat to human or animal life, it can be dangerous through long-term effects on tree roots and the foundations of buildings or other structures.

Solifluction

Solifluction is an intensified form of creep. The existence of permafrost (a layer of earth that remains in a long-term state of freeze that occurs in very cold climates) prevents absorption of surface water. The excess water then enters the topmost "active" layer of soil. That layer is thus more vulnerable to the process of creep than a comparable layer of soil in a warmer climate because of its increased fluidity and the frozen surface over which it slides. Solifluction tends to result in a "wrinkled" landscape with smooth terrain.

Water movement

The movement of water in streams and rivers plays a key role in landscape evolution. The long-term effect of rivers and streams is to erode the land around them down to sea level, the base level of erosion. There are several theories as to how this occurs:

- Backwasting entails the wearing down of river valley slopes parallel to themselves. When the surface between valley slopes is worn down to the base level of erosion, the slopes retreat in parallel layers until all of the land above the widening platform is eroded to the same level.
- Downwasting is another theoretical process that explains landscape evolution. This process involves the diminishing of valley slopes through mass movements of soil and rock decomposition.
- A peneplain is the result of the erosive process of the land around streams. It is a wide, nearly flat plain of bedrock that exists just above the base level of erosion.
- A monadnock is an anomalous portion of especially tenacious rock that rises above a peneplain.

Stream deposition

Stream deposition is the last phase in the weathering and erosion process performed by water, specifically streams. Stream erosion occurs when the movement of water in a stream detaches material from the sides and bottom of the channel through which it flows. This can carve out valleys and wide, meandering streams. Streams then carry the weathered material, as well as material deposited in the stream by other erosive processes, out to sea. Streams transport sediment in three ways:

- The solid load consists of the suspended load (sediment grains of various sizes floating in the water) and the bed load (the materials dragged along the bed of a channel by the moving water).
- The bed load performs much of the erosion of the sides and bottoms of the channel. A stream's dissolved load is composed of ions produced in the chemical weathering process.
- Stream deposition occurs when the stream drops its load of sediment. This can occur due to flooding or intersection of the stream with a larger body of water.

Soil

Soil is a result of the processes of weathering and erosion. Erosion transports rock particles and ions produced by weathering and deposits those materials, along with organic matter, in unconsolidated layers. Soil, fundamental to life on Earth, varies with regional temperatures, vegetation, rock types, and rock strength: It is made up of various types and ratios of minerals, rocks, and organic materials as well as water and air. The term soil profile refers to the composition of a soil's three horizons.

Most soils possess an A horizon (a dark-colored layer made up largely of decomposed organic matter—humus), a B horizon (consisting mainly of the products of weathering, such as clay and rust-colored iron oxides), and a C horizon (made up of materials similar to the parent materials underneath). Parent materials are those thought to be present before the formation of the soil above.

Topographic map

A topographic (topo) map is a plot of a portion of land that indicates the contours of the land in that area. Elevation is the vertical distance between a point and mean sea level. Height is the vertical distance between two points (for instance, the distance between the top of a plateau and the bottom of a basin). Relief is the difference in the elevations of the highest and lowest points in a certain area. Topographic maps (or contour maps) use contour lines to connect points with equal elevations. When a particular contour line represents an elevation below the mean sea level, it is crossed with hatch marks. This type of map is basically a two-dimensional representation of three-dimensional features (with elevation as the third dimension) on the Earth's surface. When contour lines on a topographic map are drawn closely together, it indicates that the slopes in a particular geographic area are exceptionally steep. Evenly spaced contour lines indicate a uniform sloping angle. Topographic maps are created from aerial photographs and fieldwork.

Topographic profile

A topographic profile is a representation of the skyline of a particular area (a profile line) on a topographic map. In contrast to topolographic maps, topological profiles are viewed horizontally. Creating a topolographic profile involves plotting the elevations of contour lines that cross a profile line and connecting these points to construct a cohesive profile. Artists often employ vertical exaggeration (a difference in horizontal and vertical scales on a profile) in creation of a topographic profile to highlight certain features. A true profile exists when the vertical and horizontal scales used in its production are equal.

Geologic map

Unlike a topographic map, which represents landforms on the Earth's surface, a geologic map represents rock or mineral ore formations that exist underneath the surface. An outcrop is a portion of a formation that is exposed at the surface, usually due to weathering and erosion. Often, outcrops are blanketed by sediment, soil, and/or vegetation. A contact is a plane that separates two rock formations. On a geologic map, common rock types (such as limestone, shale, and granite) are represented by graphic patterns or colors. Lines are used to delineate contact planes. Cartographers (those who draw maps) use certain symbols to indicate the presence of horizontal beds, vertical beds, axes in folded rocks, and so on. These maps are extremely useful in the location and recovery of mineral resources and fossil fuels. These formations are identified through analysis of field research data and aerial photography.

Geological cross section

A geological cross section is created through the addition of geologic information to a topographic profile. Geologists often construct maps that display both topographic and geologic information. Working from one of these maps, it is fairly easy to create a geological cross section. After a topological profile has been plotted, one may add information about subsurface rock structures and compositions underneath the profile line. This process is complicated when rock beds are folded, tilted, or faulted from their horizontal orientation. Vertical exaggeration, which can be useful in the construction of topographic profiles, should not be used in geological cross sections—employment of such a technique would distort the angles and shapes of the represented rock beds.

Stratigraphic correlation

The law of superposition states that in bodies of undisturbed sedimentary rocks, the strata at the bottom are older than the strata at the top. Stratigraphic correlation is a method used to determine the "correct" or natural stratigraphic position of rock beds which have been separated by disturbances such as metamorphic processes, orogenies, or plutonic formations. This is achieved through the identification of correspondence between two points in a characteristic such as fossil content, lithology (the physical characteristics of a rock), or geologic age. This practice of (theoretically) realigning beds which have been deformed is helpful in identification of the relative ages of rocks in a sedimentary rock sequence.

Geologic time

Geologic time may be measured absolutely using chronometric time, or relatively using chronostratic time. Measurements of chronometric time are achieved through radiometric dating and are expressed numerically in number of years. Chronostratic time, which places events in sequences, can be estimated through the study of rock bodies. According to the law of original horizontality, the original orientation of sedimentary beds is nearly always horizontal. Therefore, if one observes deformed or slanted strata, the event which disoriented the strata must have occurred after the strata was deposited. Also, a rock body that cuts across another must be newer than the rock body it intersects. Similarly, for a layer of rock to experience erosion and weathering, it must already exist on the surface. These destructive processes can lead to interruptions in the geologic record. Sometimes, sediments are deposited atop a weathered and eroded surface. Such an occurrence is called an unconformity. The most common method used to establish chronostratic time is through stratigraphy, as the name suggests.

Relative geologic time is divided into different units, including two recognized eons: the Precambrian, of which little is known due to limited fossil evidence that only reveals ultra-primitive life forms; and the Phanerozoic, for which fossil evidence is more abundant and reveals more evolved life forms. Eons are the largest units of geologic time.

P mc

Scientists also recognize three eras: the Paleozoic, the Mesozoic, and the Cenozoic. Eras contain periods, and periods contain epochs. These units are delineated largely by the conceptions used to divide historical time. They are arranged in a sequence through chronostratigraphy and classified largely on the basis of the fossils found in their associated strata.

Record of the earth's history

Eon   Eo
Era   Er
Period EP
Epoch

Rocks

One important way in which rocks provide a record of earth's history is through the study of fossils, which allows scientists to make inferences about the evolution of life on earth. However, the presentation of fossils is certainly not the only record of earth's history contained in rocks. For instance, the chemical composition of rock strata may give indications about the atmospheric and/or hydrospheric compositions at certain points in earth's history. Paleomagnetism constitutes another aspect of earth's historical record contained in rocks. Through the study of magnetic orientations of rocks formed at certain times in history, scientists learn more about the form and function of earth's magnetic field then and now.

Sediments

The study of the sediments which make up sedimentary rocks can reveal much about the environment in which they are formed. For example, a study of the different types of sediments in a bed, and the ratios in which they occur, can indicate the types of rocks exposed at the origination site and the relative abundances of each. Examination of the sorting of a sediment can reveal information about how far the particles traveled from their provenance, as well as the medium which carried the particles. For example, sediments transported by wind tend to be well-sorted, while water moves large particles which are often worn into spheres. The type of weathering experienced by particles in a sedimentary bed can reveal the climate from which they came—mechanical weathering tends to occur in cold and arid climates, while chemical weathering is more common in hot and humid climates. Interpreting the information supplied by sediment can, in turn, reveal information about past conditions on earth.

water

Cold mechanical
hot Chemistry

Soil

The study of soil development can give indications of the age of certain sedimentary deposits. For example, the study of soil led to the idea that multiple glaciations have occurred on the North American continent. Examination of the development level of certain areas of soil can also inform earth scientists about natural catastrophic events which have occurred in the past. Study of soil deposits also aided in the determination of how often "ice ages" can be expected to occur. Also, the presence of certain types of soil buried deep beneath the surface can provide indications of past climates.

Radiometric dating

Radiometric dating is one of the only methods currently available to determine the absolute age of an object such as a fossil or rock body. This process is possible when such an object contains isotopes, the products of radioactive decay. In radioactive decay, the atoms of certain unstable isotopes are transformed through the emissions of either electrons or alpha particles. This process occurs exponentially until it produces a stable final product. The rate of radioactive decay is measured in half-lives: after one half-life has passed, one-half of the atoms of the original element will have decayed. When scientists examine an object which contains isotopes with known half-life periods, they can determine the amount of the isotope that was present at the time of the object's origin. That figure can then be compared with the present level to determine the age of the object.

% C in a body

how can they know how much was originally prese

Precambrian Eon

There is comparatively little evidence to support much elaboration about the environment during the Precambrian time. However, enough is known to divide the eon into three eras. During the earliest Hadean era, which occurred 4.5 to 3.8 billion years ago, the solar system was formed. The earliest microfossils date to the Archaean era about 3.8 to 2.5 billion years ago and reveal the existence of cyanobacteria, photosynthetic organisms which produced oxygen as a byproduct. During the Proterozoic era of 2.5 billion to 543 million years ago, the fossil record indicates an abundance of bacteria as well as the appearance of eukaryotic cells. Fossil soils known as paleosols also reveal high levels of metal oxides, indicating that the oxygen levels in the atmosphere were extremely high, probably due to the presence of many cyanobacteria. Fossil dating also proves the emergence of the first animals, called Vendian animals, from late in this era, roughly 650 to 543 million years ago.

has O_2 decreased?

Phanerozoic

Paleozoic Era

The Paleozoic Era, which occurred 543 to 248 million years ago, dominates nearly half of the Phanerozoic eon. The era began with a huge increase in the diversity of multicellular organisms. Animals, plants, fungi, and insects all experienced rapid evolution during this time. During the early part of this era, marine animals such as trilobites and brachiopods were abundant. Life on land began to proliferate approximately 440 to 425 million years ago, beginning with plants and expanding to include invertebrates and vertebrates. The presence of limestone outcrops provides evidence of changing sea levels during this era; massive coal deposits also formed during this time. Also, the supercontinent Pangaea came together towards the end of the Paleozoic Era. Earth's climate became warmer and drier during this time, which coincided with a decrease in glacial activity. This era concluded with the most massive extinction event in history. The event's cause is uncertain, but it is known to have eliminated 90 percent of the planet's living marine species.

2. **Mesozoic Era**

The Mesozoic Era, which occurred 248 to 65 million years ago, was the age of the dinosaurs—they evolved at the beginning of the era and all but birds were extinct by its end. The famous K-T extinction event eliminated 85 percent of all species. This period of time exhibited flora and fauna which were very different from those of the Paleozoic Era. Pangaea began to break apart during the Triassic period, and mammals evolved from a line of "mammal-like reptiles." The Jurassic period saw the emergence of the first birds, as well as a proliferation of crocodiles, sharks, and rays. The first flowering plants evolved during the Cretaceous period. By the time this period began, Pangea had broken into several smaller continents. At the end of this period around 65 million years ago, a massive asteroid hit what is now Mexico's Yucatan Peninsula. Whether the asteroid caused the K-T extinction event, however, is debatable.

3. **Cenozoic Era**

The Cenozoic Era, which began 65 million years ago and reaches to the present, is subdivided into six epochs delineated by the percentage of fossilized species living at the time of classification in several strata of rocks. Though this naming process occurred in a single area, it has been correlated worldwide. Therefore, unlike the relatively arbitrary subdivisions of other eras, the subdivisions of this era are based on practical experience. The oldest known fossils of modern species date to this period; these species evolved into the forms which are recognized today. The exposure of the Panamanian land bridge spread species across the continents. Homo sapiens evolved and became dominant during this modern period, which also saw the most recent ice age. Fossils from the Cenozoic Era are abundant and of high-quality. As a result, more is known about the flora, fauna, and environmental conditions during this era than any other. Some people also recognize a seventh epoch, the Holocene, which covers the last 11,000 years.

Gaia hypothesis

Named for the Greek goddess who organized a living earth from chaos, the Gaia hypothesis states that the planet is a living system. While this idea is not scientific in the literal sense, it provides a metaphor which is useful in achieving an understanding of the interconnectedness of all of earth's systems. For example, increased levels of carbon dioxide in the atmosphere breed higher levels of plant growth, and these plants help to regulate the amount of carbon dioxide present in the atmosphere. Feedback mechanisms such as this were known before the formulation of the Gaia hypothesis. However, adherence to this idea requires one to study the planet as a whole, rather than focusing on only one of its many aspects in isolation. The fact that earth's atmosphere is quite different from those of the other planets led to the formulation of this idea.

Origination of Earth

Many different theories have been advanced regarding the birth of the planet. The theory which is currently most accepted, the nebular hypothesis, involves the formation of a cloud of dust and gas around the sun, probably due to one or more supernovae. The sun formed from such a cloud of gas and dust, collapsing in on itself through gravitational compaction. Once formed, nuclear fusion of hydrogen began in its core, producing heat and light. Next, other particles derived from the huge supernova began to coalesce, also due to gravitational forces. These accretions of material are called planetesimals. These bodies continued to compact, forming the nine planets of the solar system. The extreme heat which must have been present during these events indicates that Earth, like the other planets, must have been completely molten at its birth. When it finally began to cool, its constituent elements solidified into rocks.

Darwin's theory of evolution

Darwin's book *On the Origin of Species* gave us a unifying concept in science. Darwin offered two theories:
- The theory of evolution states that all living things have evolved from common ancestors over millions of years. They diverged into multiple species gradually through a process of change and variation.
- The theory of natural selection concludes that changes in natural conditions select stronger organisms, while less-adaptable organisms tend not to survive and, therefore, fail to contribute to future generations. The key issue of survival is successful reproduction.

The theory of evolution explains both the unity and diversity of life: Many organisms share common traits yet show great diversity. The accumulated evidence for the theory of evolution is overwhelming: Almost all scientists consider evolution a scientific fact.

Life

A good working definition of life is a group of processes that results from a complex organization of matter. Life is a sum of varied processes and structures observed in organisms as simple as a cell or as complex as man. All of life shares certain qualities:
- Living things have a complex organization.
- Living things take in and use energy.
- Living things grow and develop.
- Living things show variation through heredity.

- Living things possess a genetic code that ensures future generations.
- Living things are able to adapt to their environments.
- Living things respond to stimuli.

Modern view of the origin of life

It is believed that complex chemicals generated by the heat of the sun and other factors caused the creation of simple atoms and molecules. These chemicals are thought to have caused the bonding of simple structures into primitive, organized systems able to reproduce themselves. These were the first cells—the beginning of life on Earth. Mutations in the genetic code of cells resulted in variations of new cells that ultimately created a huge variety of species, becoming more complex and specialized over a long span of time.

Living entities and nonliving matter

The elemental components most commonly found in living organisms (hydrogen, oxygen, carbon, nitrogen, sulfur, and phosphorus) are common throughout the universe. However, the chemistry of carbon displayed in living beings is unique. Also, the organic compounds (proteins, certain sugars, and nucleic acids necessary in protein synthesis and the storage and transmission of genetic information) found in live organisms are not found in inorganic matter. Presently on earth, there are no observable instances of the spontaneous generation of these compounds in nonliving matter. Another important factor which distinguishes live organisms from those which are not alive is the ability of life to reproduce itself. Also, organic beings possess the unique ability to react to external stimuli.

Biogenesis and abiogenesis

Biogenesis is the process of life emerging from life. Modern science has never observed any instance in which life can arise from nonliving materials; rather, all modern organisms are produced by other living organisms like themselves. In a narrower sense, biogenesis is the basis of creation biology, which holds that since life must be created from life, a god figure must have created the earliest life forms on Earth.

Abiogenesis is an oppositional process: the creation of life from nonliving matter. The ancient version of abiogenesis involved the generation of complex, fully-formed organisms from nonliving matter; for example, the creation of mice from putrefying wood. The modern definition of the term is generally applied to the evolution of modern life from simple organisms created by the interactions of nonliving chemicals in the early atmosphere and hydrosphere, although the processes by which this occurred are largely unknown.

Life's last common ancestor

Louis Pasteur disproved the hypothesis of the spontaneous generation of life through his work with bacteria; he proved that even microorganisms are bred from "parents" with similar attributes. The work of Charles Darwin demonstrated that complex organisms evolve from simpler ones by the process of natural selection. Taken together, these scientific discoveries suggest that all of the life currently on Earth could have evolved from a single, simple, original organism—"life's last common ancestor." This organism must have possessed the capabilities to store information regarding function and reproduction in nucleic acids and to replicate that information with random variations which would have led to the development of different traits. This ancestor must have been constituted of carbon-rich elements and must have contained proteins formed of one set of 20 amino acids, including enzymes to spawn vital processes.

Miller-Urey experiment

The Miller-Urey experiment, performed at the University of Chicago in 1953 by Harold Urey and Stanley Miller, proved that prebiotic chemistry could have produced amino acids, the basic molecules of life. Chemicals thought to have been present in the atmosphere of early Earth (methane, hydrogen, water, and ammonia) were introduced into a glass bulb to replicate the atmosphere. Another bulb was filled with water to simulate the ocean; this bulb was heated to replicate the effect of the sun. The two bulbs were connected with tubing, which allowed evaporated material in the "atmosphere" to return to the "ocean." Electrodes in the tubing exposed this primordial soup to "lightning." After a few weeks had passed, the two men analyzed the liquid in the contraption, and discovered that the chemical reactions which had taken place produced several amino acids, indicating the feasibility of the creation of molecules basic to life by prebiotic chemistry. These molecules could have accumulated and led to the chemical evolution of increasingly complex life forms.

Alternate theories for formation of molecules of life

Some scientists have theorized that the basic molecules of life may have arrived on Earth from an extraterrestrial source. A carbonaceous meteorite, which hit Australia several years after the Miller-Urey experiment, was found to contain the same amino acids produced by the experiment in roughly the same proportions. The purine bases of nucleic acids (adenine and guanine) have been shown to exist in meteorites as well. Also, complex molecules vital to life on Earth have been detected in a nebula. Clay theory suggests that organic molecules arose progressively from the "replication platform" of silicate crystals in solution.

RNA world hypothesis

The RNA world hypothesis attempts to explain the development of protocells from simple organic molecules. This hypothesis is a "gene first" hypothesis, meaning that it represents the view that nucleic acids formed before the biochemical reactions and pathways required for self-replication existed. The RNA world hypothesis suggests that nucleotides, the units from which RNA strands are formed, floated in the primordial soup along with other chemicals. Eventually, some of these nucleotides were synthesized into chains, which are said to be the first forms of life. These primitive life forms would have then engaged in competition for free nucleotides; this competition operated as a process of natural selection. The RNA chains then developed the ability to link amino acids into proteins and continued to evolve into the first prokaryotic cells. The discovery that RNA could behave as an enzyme (a ribozyme) lent credence to the idea that RNA could catalyze protein synthesis. Some discredit this hypothesis because there is little evidence that nucleotides could have been formed in the primordial soup.

Iron-sulfur world theory

The iron-sulfur world theory is a "metabolism first" model of the evolution of organic molecules into primitive cells—it suggests that the formation of primitive metabolism (a cycle of energy-producing chemical reactions) created an environment in which RNA could later form. The energy produced by these reactions could in turn fuel the development of increasingly complex cells. This hypothesis states that organic molecules were created on the surfaces of iron-bearing minerals near hydrothermal vents on the ocean floor, rather than in the "soup" of the ocean itself. Redox reactions of metal sulfides may have provided the energy necessary for development of self-replicating organisms. This model is attractive because it provides for a succession of developmental steps within a single structure. Critics, however, have pointed out that the spontaneous development of a closed metabolic cycle such as that included in the iron-sulfur theory is unlikely.

Evolution

Evolution is the process whereby organisms pass certain acquired traits to successive generations, affecting the attributes of later organisms and even leading to the creation of new species. Charles Darwin is the name often associated with the formulation of natural selection, a vital component of evolution as it is known today. Natural selection states that members of a species are not identical—due to their respective genetic make-ups, each individual will possess traits which make it stronger or weaker and more or less able to adapt. The other tenet of natural selection is that members of a species will always have to compete for scarce resources to survive. Therefore, organisms with traits which will help them survive are more likely to do so and produce offspring, passing along the "desirable" traits. Darwin suggested that this process, by creating groups of a species with increasingly different characteristics, would eventually lead to the formation of a new species. The fossil record has provided support for this theory.

Significant events leading to evolution of man

The origination of life is the most fundamental development in the history of life on Earth. Prokaryotic microfossils, the earliest fossils identified by paleontologists, are dated to near 3.5 billion years ago. However, the presence of large amounts of certain carbon and oxygen isotopes in sedimentary rocks dated at about 3.8 billion years ago may indicate the presence of organic material. The next significant event suggested by a drastic change in the fossil record is the huge diversification of species which occurred approximately 543 million years ago, near the end of the Precambrian eon and the beginning of the Phanerozoic. This evolutionary stage included higher-level tissue organization in multicellular organisms, the development of predator-prey relationships, and, most importantly, the development of skeletons. The final critical step toward the evolution of man is the emergence of life on land about 418 million years ago. This necessitated the evolution of structures which could breathe air, obtain and retain water on land, and support its own weight out of water.

Organism species classification

The study of the evolutionary relationships between organism species is called phylogenetics. In this field of study, scientists make use of cladistic taxonomy to classify species. Cladistic taxonomy places species in groups based on "shared derived properties" called synamorphies, which are physical similarities assumed to be shared by different species because they evolved from a common ancestor. In this method, organism species are placed in successively smaller cladistic groups, originally delineated by Carolus Linnaeus. The divisions of this five-kingdom system are, from broadest to narrowest: Kingdom, Phylum, Class, Order, Family, Genus, and Species. Phylogenetic classification can be expressed graphically through a phylogenetic, or evolutionary, tree. Some modern scientists adhere to the recently developed three-domain system, which features a top-level grouping of domain consisting of Archaea, Eukaryota, and Eubacteria.

Biochemical record and imperfect design

Biochemical record refers to the genetic coding of organisms. This information may be examined in one organism and compared to that of another. The theory of evolution suggests that modern-day organisms should share certain aspects of their genetic codes due to the fact that certain organisms, like humans and apes, share common ancestors. Therefore, investigation of this biochemical record reveals that the closer organisms are on the evolutionary tree, the more similar their DNA will be. Organisms do not need to be perfect to survive, only better than their competitors. Thus, the attributes of each member of an evolved species builds on those of the organisms before it. This means that certain traits which may have

- 54 -

been optimal in the past get cemented into the genetic make-up of a species, even if "better" ones are currently available. This is called imperfect design, a phenomenon that lends support to the theory of evolution while contradicting the deterministic the belief that each organism exists for a specific purpose.

Resources

A resource is a commodity that is useful or necessary to sustain life and/or the industries and lifestyles of global societies. Natural resources are Earth materials that can be used to further those ends. A renewable resource is one that may be replenished after use and will therefore be available in the long term. A nonrenewable resource is one that is permanently depleted after its currently available supply has been exhausted. Recovery of a paramarginal resource is feasible, given current technological capabilities, though not exceptionally profitable (the main incentive to recover any resource is an economic one). Recovery of a submarginal resource is not profitable—it would cost more in energy and financial resources to recover such a resource than such recovery would provide (the cost of recovery outweighs the potential benefits of recovery). The reserve of a resource is the estimated amount of that resource that is recoverable with current technological capabilities; this amount is usually a fraction of the total amount of the resource.

Natural resources can be minerals, fossil fuels, animals, or plants. Mineral resources are often metal elements. For instance, iron and manganese are used in steel production. Lead is used in the manufacture of batteries and gasoline. Silver is used as currency; it is also an important material in photographic film. Fossil fuels, such as petroleum (oil and gas) and coal, are used to produce energy for indoor climate control and to power industrial plants and automobiles. Fossil fuels are also vital to agricultural processes, which produce food and cotton. Animals are used as food (for example, fish) or to produce materials like leather for clothing. Plants are also consumed as food. Wood is a valuable resource used in the construction of buildings and furniture.

Igneous processes may result in the deposition of ore resources. For example, liquid differentiation and crystallization within magma may lead to the deposition of minerals rich in iron and titanium (relatively abundant resources) or copper (a relatively rare ore used in the construction of electrical wiring). Contact metamorphism is another geological process with the ability to produce natural resources. Limestone is a common host rock for the formation of oxides of zinc (an anticorrosive alloy) and copper through this process. The sedimentation of mineral particles in pockets along water bodies can lead to the formation of gold deposits; this was the case during the Gold Rush. Weathering processes may lead to ore deposition in humid climates, where soluble elements such as magnesium are evaporated from soil, leaving deposits of insoluble elements such as iron and nickel.

Problems with use of natural resources

The world's population and the average consumption of resources are increasing exponentially. The main problem with the use of natural resources, such as mineral ores, is that those materials take hundreds of thousands or even millions of years to form. Igneous, sedimentary, metamorphic, and weathering processes occur on such large time scales that reliance on these mechanisms for resource production would be unrealistic even if global levels of resource consumption were not rising so quickly. Also, the geological processes that produce these resources are not evenly distributed across the globe; total reliance on these elements would entail the same difficulties bred by unevenly distributed oil reserves.

Crude oil

Oil is produced when liquid and gaseous organic materials are involved in complex chemical reactions and then migrate into the pore space of sedimentary rocks. This process takes thousands or millions of years to complete. One problem with the use of oil as a natural resource is that we are completely unsure of the amount of oil that will be available for human consumption in the future. Technology, though it has improved over the years, is still incapable of examining every possible location for the presence of usable oil. Also, the uneven distribution of the global oil supply has the potential to problematize the attainment of oil, both politically and economically. Finally, the recovery of oil comes with high energy expenditures, as well as the danger of causing pollution and destroying local vegetation.

Fossil fuels

Coal, natural gas, and petroleum are all fossil fuels. Each of these energy sources contains potential energy received from the Sun. To release the stored energy, the fuel must be burned. This process changes the stored energy into heat energy. That heat energy, in turn, can be used to create electrical power or to produce heat for indoor climate control. One problem with the use of fossil fuels lies in the fact that fuel combustion creates by-products, such as carbon dioxide, that adversely affect Earth's atmosphere. Another problem with fossils fuels lies in their limited availability.

Burning fossil fuels (naturally-occurring hydrocarbon compounds that may be used by humans for fuel), especially coal, releases harmful elements into the atmosphere. The chemical reaction of coal combustion produces, for example, large amounts of carbon dioxide. When these gases reach the atmosphere, they inhibit the release of infrared photons into space—carbon dioxide molecules absorb the photons and may reflect them inward, back toward the Earth. This phenomenon is called the greenhouse effect. While the greenhouse effect is desirable, to a certain degree, to maintain a comfortable climate on the planet, increased levels of carbon dioxide can change the balance of energy in the atmosphere. This is termed global warming. Coal burning can also cause acid rain. Sulfur dioxide, a byproduct of burning coal, rises to the atmosphere and combines with water molecules to form sulfuric acid. This acid rain falls back to Earth, where it can cause harm to plants, animals, water bodies, and exposed structures. Burning gasoline can also contribute to the formation of acid rain.

Renewable energy

Wind, hydroelectric, and geothermal power are renewable energy sources. In wind and hydroelectric power, the motion of wind and water, respectively, are used to turn rotors called turbines. The motion of the turbines is converted by generators into electric power. Geothermal power is created by nuclear reactions in the Earth's core. Those reactions create heat, which travels below the Earth's surface in the form of water or magma. This heat energy is sometimes released through hot springs or geysers on the Earth's surface. Geothermal power can be used for indoor climate control or, like water and wind, to power electric generators.

Important terms

Chronostratigraphy - an aspect of stratigraphy which focuses on the relative ages of geologic strata. Scientists examine the physical interrelations of strata, the relations of strata to the sequence of organic evolution, and radioactive ages of strata to determine their chronological sequence. When the relative ages of strata have been identified, scientists can examine the constituents and properties of those strata for clues about the sequence of events which made the world what it is today.

Geological stratum - a layer of rock which possesses certain attributes which distinguishes it from adjacent layers of rock. Such attributes include, but are not limited to, lithology, chemical composition, and mineralogy.

Stratigraphy - the study of the arrangement, form, distribution, composition, and succession of rock strata. Information gained from such study is then used to form hypotheses about the strata's origins, environments, relations to organic environments, relations to other geologic concepts, and ages.

Oceanography and Freshwater Systems

Water molecule

The water molecule consists of two hydrogen atoms and one oxygen atom (H_2O). The atoms in this molecule are joined through covalent bonding. The two hydrogen-oxygen bonds are at a 105-degree angle from each other, rather than on opposite sides of the oxygen atom. The water molecule has a positive charge on the hydrogen side and a negative charge on the oxygen side. The electrons in the hydrogen atoms are so strongly attracted to the oxygen atom that they are actually closer to the oxygen atom's nucleus than to the nuclei of the hydrogen atoms. This asymmetrical arrangement of atoms in the water molecule characterizes it as a polar molecule. This polar quality is the force that causes water molecules to bond so readily with other water molecules; water is a good solvent because of its polar structure.

Specific heat in water

The heat capacity of a substance is defined as the amount of heat required to raise the temperature of a given amount of the substance one degree; it thus describes the ability of a substance to store heat. The specific heat of a substance is its heat capacity per unit of mass. Specific heat is often expressed as calorie per gram degree Celsius. The specific heat of water is 1 cal/g degree Celsius. This specific heat is much higher than that of most other substances. Water exhibits this unique property due to its atomic structure. Hydrogen bonding, like that in a water molecule, releases heat, and heat absorption is required to break hydrogen bonds. Thus, one additional calorie of heat causes a small change in the temperature of water because the heat energy is put toward dissolving the hydrogen bonds. Conversely, a slight decrease in the temperature of water is accompanied by the formation of several hydrogen bonds and the release of relatively large amounts of heat energy.

bond :
exo

break :
end

High specific heat

The high specific heat of the water molecule means that its temperature change when it absorbs or loses an amount of heat will be minimal, especially as compared to other substances. For instance, an ocean or other large body of water can store large amounts of heat from the Sun without becoming terribly hot. Also, the cooling of water bodies after the Sun goes down is accompanied by a release of heat that warms the ambient air. The role that water plays in temperature regulation (both in water and on land) is vital to the maintenance of life on Earth.

Density changes in water

Water is one of few substances that is more dense in its liquid form than it is in its solid form. Fresh (uncontaminated) water is densest at four degrees Celsius. At temperatures above this point, water expands as it warms and contracts as it cools, like other liquid substances. At temperatures below four degrees Celsius, however, water expands as it cools. As it cools from this temperature, water molecules slow to the point at which hydrogen bonds can form. At zero degrees Celsius, the molecules are oriented into a crystalline structure, in which hydrogen bonding keeps them equally spaced at distances far enough apart to make ice less dense than water. Again, this unusual property of water is vital to life on Earth. If, like most substances, the solid form of water was denser than the liquid form, entire oceans would freeze when ice sank; only the top few feet of water would thaw during hot weather. Since this is not the case, however, ice floats, insulating the water below and thus preventing it from freezing.

Cohesion-tension theory

The cohesion-tension theory was advanced to explain the method of transport of water from the roots of a plant, where it receives its water supply, to its uppermost leaves, even in the tallest trees. Hydrogen bonds in water molecules form strong bonds with the oxygen atoms in all nearby water molecules. Water moves from plant cells into leaf pores one molecule at a time. As one molecule exits a cell, another water molecule from lower in the plant enters the same cell. This movement, caused by the cohesive properties of the water molecule, creates a tension among all of the (connected) water molecules in the plant and even those in the soil about to enter the plant's roots. This tension provides the force needed to move water upward through a plant from its roots.

Hydrologic cycle

The hydrologic (water) cycle refers to the circulation of water in the Earth's hydrosphere (below the surface, on the surface, and above the surface of the Earth). This continuous process involves five physical actions. Evaporation entails the change of water molecules from a liquid to gaseous state. Liquid water on the Earth's surface (often contained in a large body of water) becomes water vapor and enters the atmosphere when its component molecules gain enough kinetic (heat) energy to escape the liquid form. As the vapor rises, it cools and therefore loses its ability to maintain the gaseous form. It begins to the process of condensation (the return to a liquid or solid state) and forms clouds. When the clouds become sufficiently dense, the water falls back to Earth as precipitation. Water is then either trapped in vegetation (interception) or absorbed into the surface (infiltration). Runoff, caused by gravity, physically moves water downward into oceans or other water bodies.

Evaporation is the change of state in a substance from a liquid to a gaseous form at a temperature below its boiling point (the temperature at which all of the molecules in a liquid are changed to gas through vaporization). Some of the molecules at the surface of a liquid always maintain enough heat energy to escape the cohesive forces exerted on them by neighboring molecules. At higher temperatures, the molecules in a substance move more rapidly, increasing their number with enough energy to break out of the liquid form. The rate of evaporation is higher when more of the surface area of a liquid is exposed (as in a large water body, such as an ocean). The amount of moisture already in the air also affects the rate of evaporation—if there is a significant amount of water vapor in the air around a liquid, some evaporated molecules will return to the liquid. The speed of the evaporation process is also decreased by increased atmospheric pressure.

Condensation is the phase change in a substance from a gaseous to liquid form; it is the opposite of evaporation or vaporization. When temperatures decrease in a gas, such as water vapor, the material's component molecules move more slowly. The decreased motion of the molecules enables intermolecular cohesive forces to pull the molecules closer together and, in water, establish hydrogen bonds. Condensation can also be caused by an increase in the pressure exerted on a gas, which results in a decrease in the substance's volume (it reduces the distance between particles). In the hydrologic cycle, this process is initiated when warm air containing water vapor rises and then cools. This occurs due to convection in the air, meteorological fronts, or lifting over high land formations.

In the hydrologic cycle, the principal movement of water in the atmosphere is its transport from the area above an ocean to an area over land. If this transport did not occur, the hydrologic cycle would be less a cycle than the vertical motion of water from the oceans to the atmosphere and back again. Some evaporated water is transported in the form of clouds consisting of condensed water droplets and small ice crystals. The clouds are moved by the jetstream (strong winds in the upper levels of the atmosphere that are related to surface temperatures) or by surface winds (land or sea breezes). Most of the water that moves through the atmosphere is water vapor (water in the gaseous form).

Surface tension of water

Cohesive forces are attractive forces that act between the molecules of a liquid. In most areas of a liquid, the molecules experience these forces equally from all directions. On the surface of a liquid, however, the molecules are drawn inward toward the center of the liquid's mass but experience no equal force from the outside. This causes the surface to contract and behave like a stretched elastic membrane. This property of a liquid is referred to as its surface tension. Water has a relatively high surface tension; this means that it forms stable, spherical droplets when placed on a nonsoluble surface. The high surface tension of water is what allows denser objects to float and insects (such as the water skater) to walk atop water bodies.

Role of water in maintenance of life

Living entities need water to live. This is because of the important role of water, often called the universal solvent, in facilitating vital chemical reactions within organisms. Living things are made up of molecules suspended in aqueous solutions (substances dissolved in water), and cells are 70–90% water. Thus, the ability of organic molecules to interact with water affects their functions. The reactions between compounds enabled by the presence of water molecules fuel metabolic and digestive processes, as well as processes of cell replication. In addition, organic compounds within a body can be transported in water due to its high surface tension.

Earth's hydrosphere

The collective mass of water found on and beneath the Earth's surface known as the hydrosphere was formed from the same processes which formed the Earth's atmosphere. Basically, outgassing from the Earth's mantle through volcanic eruptions thrust steam into the atmosphere. Water molecules then condensed high above the Earth as clouds, which then rained liquid water back to the surface. While the planet was too hot in its earliest stages to sustain liquid water on its surface, the water molecules simply returned to a gaseous form, evaporated back into the atmosphere, and began the cycle anew. Eventually, around 3.3 billion years ago, the planet cooled enough to allow water to remain on the surface in the crustal depressions created during the compaction and cooling processes. Large volumes of rain eventually formed oceans. Later, water weathering and erosion created multitudinous channels, both on the surface and below it, through which the water could flow.

Distribution

Water covers about 70% of the Earth's surface; it exists under the surface in aquifers; on the surface in oceans, seas, rivers, lakes, and within organisms; and above the surface as clouds, water vapor, and precipitation. Large water bodies such as oceans hold about 97.5% of the Earth's water supply. Approximately 2.4% of that supply is contained within the lithosphere, and less than 0.001% of the Earth's water is in the atmosphere at any given time. The total amount of water in the Earth system remains constant, despite the fact that water levels in any particular location fluctuate constantly. Conservation of this water supply is performed through the functions of the water, or hydrologic, cycle.

Prehistoric oceans

The elements present in the earliest oceans were quite different from those present in the Earth's hydrosphere today. This is largely due to the chemical composition of the atmosphere at that time. The oceans were formed when cooling caused atmospheric clouds to condense and produce rain. Volcanic gasses contributed elements such as sulfur and carbon dioxide to the air. Therefore, scientists suspect that the earliest oceans contained high levels of acids (for example, sulfuric acid, hydrochloric acid, and hydrofluoric acid), and low levels of the salts that inhabit the oceans today. The temperature in this early ocean was probably close to 100 degrees Celsius. As carbon dioxide began to dissolve in the water, it combined with carbonate ions to form limestone which was deposited on the ocean floor. Consequently, more carbon dioxide was trapped in these rocks. Eventually, calcium carbonate began to reduce the acidity of these early oceans. Weathering brought different minerals into the ocean, which began to increase its saltiness toward its current levels.

Chemical composition of oceans

Salinity is the proportion of salts (inorganic minerals) dissolved in the ocean. These minerals are present as ions within seawater. The proportions of the minerals most commonly found in seawater are as follows: chloride (55%); sodium (31%); sulfate (8%); magnesium (4%); calcium and potassium (1% each); bromide, boric acid, bicarbonate, fluoride, and strontium (less than 1% each). While seawater's salinity may vary, the proportion of salt minerals remains constant. Carbon dioxide, nitrogen, and oxygen are present as dissolved gases in the oceans. The nutrients dissolved in seawater include nitrogen, phosphorus, and silica. The salinity of the oceans is affected by weathering and erosive processes of rocks on land by precipitation (which eventually returns to the seas as runoff), volcanic emissions, and the activity at hydrothermal vents on the deep seafloor. Deep sea vents are created at locations near underwater ridges when mantle material causes the eruption of water containing minerals (such as magnesium) through the lithosphere. The salinity of the ocean affects its electrical conductivity and density.

Island arc, oceanic trench and continental shelf

An island arc is one potential result of the convergence of two oceanic plates; it is a type of archipelago (chain of islands). When one plate subducts the other, the mantle of the subducting plate is partially melted by the increase in temperature of the subducted plate, which also drives water up into the overriding plate's mantle. As the temperature of the mantle increases and absorbs water, it becomes magma riddled with dissolving gases. This low-density material enters and exits the overriding plate. This process creates volcanic chains, such as the Pacific's Ring of Fire, which go through alternate periods of high and low activity. An oceanic trench is a long, deep, narrow depression in the oceanic lithosphere. The Mariana Trench, located in the Pacific Ocean, boasts the deepest measured location: 10,911 meters below sea level. A continental shelf is the submerged edge of a continent. These shelves are often eliminated when an oceanic plate slips under a continental plate at a converging plate boundary.

A continental shelf is a portion of the ocean floor that exists as a platform shallowly submerged off of a beach. This platform has a slight downward grade; its surface is uneven, with a relief (due to glacial activity) up to 100 meters. Sediment and sedimentary rock make up most continental shelves. The surface of a continental shelf is affected by natural dams, such as tectonic dams (rocks forced upward by tectonic motion) and diapirs (domes of salt that form under sedimentary rocks and push up through the rocks). The presence of these dams creates a depression in which sediment is deposited. A continental shelf experiences an abrupt increase in slope (at an average depth of 133 meters) at the shelf break, the outer boundary of the shelf. The irregular slope that extends downward from the shelf break is called the continental slope; this transition zone connects sea level to the ocean floor (about 3,660 meters below sea level).

Submarine canyon

A submarine canyon is a steep-walled valley in a continental slope. Some believe that these canyons are formed by mass movements of rock along the slope or by turbidity currents (currents initiated by the motion of debris-filled water at the tops of the canyons). It has also been suggested that these canyons were created at a point in time when at least a portion of the relevant area was above sea level; such a point might be the lowering of sea level during the Pleistocene glaciations. These formations occur more often on steeper slopes than on slopes with gentle gradients. Submarine fans (sediment deposits that travel through the canyon and then spill out onto the seafloor), which are similar to land-bound alluvial fans, form the boundary (called the continental rise) between the continental slope and the ocean floor.

Deep seafloor

The deepest level of the seafloor, which spans from one continental margin to another, is called the abyss floor. The flat, relatively featureless aspects of this floor (which is often covered with either basaltic floods or sediment) are called abyssal plains. Abyssal hills are fairly gentle rises along the floor of the abyss. The ocean ridge system, which is tall enough in some places to break the ocean surface, stands in sharp contrast to the abyssal plains. The ridge system, including the Mid-Atlantic Ridge, includes the median rift, a long, continuous depression that follows the crest. The floor of the deep ocean also exhibits trenches (the deepest part of the ocean) and chains of volcanic islands called island arcs. Basaltic seafloor volcanoes called seamounts are reminiscent of intermediate land volcanoes. Seamounts are not tall enough to reach the ocean's surface. Guyots are enormous undersea volcanoes whose apexes appear to have been shorn off, creating a nearly level underwater shelf. Oceanographers have been unable to establish a consensus explanation of this phenomenon.

Coral reefs

A coral reef is an underwater formation composed mainly of coral (small marine creatures similar to anemones) and algae. These often-beautiful undersea features usually form in warm, clear water. They develop their own ecosystems, composed of a wide variety of plant and animal species. Before he became (in)famous for his theory of genetic evolution, Charles Darwin spent time during an ocean voyage studying (among other things) coral reefs. He identified three major varieties of reef and postulated a successive relationship between them: A fringing reef (which extends out from and grows along a shoreline) begins to grow around a sinking volcanic island. The fringing reef becomes a barrier reef surrounding the still-sinking island when the portion of the reef closest to the shore cannot keep up with the biotic (live) growth of the outer potion; the inner portion becomes a lagoon. This process continues, and the reef continues to spread around the island in a circuit. When the island sinks completely, the coral formation has become an atoll.

Sediments on the ocean floor

Much of the abyss floor is covered with sediment. The amount of sediment in any location on the ocean floor is related to the age of that portion of the oceanic lithosphere. Ooze is a type of sediment that accumulates over time from fragments of deceased surface organisms. The type of ooze deposited varies with depth and chemical conditions. Calcareous ooze is ooze made up mostly of the carbonate remains of organisms such as shells. This type of material dissolves at depths below four kilometers. Siliceous ooze is that composed of the remains of silica-cell–producing organisms. This type of ooze also dissolves under certain conditions; however, it is more resistant to dissolution than carbonate material. Sediment at the deepest levels of the ocean consists largely of (inorganic) clay, with the occasional appearance of fossils like sharks' teeth. Oceanic sediments provide large amounts of information about the Earth's prehistory, due to its sheer volume and the fact that fossils survive better undersea (without oxygen) than fossils on land.

Seafloor spreading

Radiometric dating of fossils found in basins on the ocean floor have revealed that that crust is several million years younger than the continental crust. This can be explained by the phenomenon of seafloor spreading. As undersea subduction zones are created at convergent boundaries, aspects of the oceanic lithosphere are destroyed when they are forced down into the mantle. The destruction of this crust requires the formation of new crustal material elsewhere, since the diameter of the Earth is not changing. At divergent boundaries, seafloor spreading occurs. When portions of the crust move apart, mantle materials flood up and harden to form new crust. Therefore, the apparent discrepancies in between the age of the ocean floor as revealed by radiometric dating and the age of the oceans as suggested by paleoclimatology can be explained by the fact that new crust is continually being created on the ocean floor at zones of seafloor spreading.

Sea breezes

The daily influxes in the strength and direction of wind at ocean coasts are collectively referred to as sea breezes. These phenomena contribute to the climatemediating function of oceanic bodies. When solar energy hits the coastal surface during a sunny day, the ground warms quickly. Air above this heated land rises through convection, creating a low-pressure zone. Cooler air then flows into the region vacated by the risen air, creating a cool onshore breeze (unlike meteorologists, oceanographers name winds for the direction they are headed) by the middle of the day. Conversely, when the shore cools after the Sun goes down, the air above it cools and sinks. The direction of wind flow is then reversed, creating an offshore breeze in the evening.

Seawater motion and atmospheric wind patterns

We can envision the ocean as a series of layers of water, loosely connected to one another by friction. Winds over the ocean move the surface layer of water, which exerts a force on the layer below it, which affects the layer below it, and so on. However, the energy generated by the wind decreases with ocean depth, so that after a certain point (usually a depth of 100–200 meters), the wind has little if any effect on the water. Due to the influence of the Coriolis force, surface currents do not move in the same direction as the winds above it; ocean waves seem to move to the right of the wind in the area. This can be explained in terms of Ekman transport. This theory states that as each layer of oceanic water is touched by wind, it also experiences the effects of the Coriolis force, which causes it to move 90 degrees to the right (or left, in the Southern Hemisphere) and spiral downward (an Ekman spiral).

Seawater circulation

At the surface, atmospheric winds and the Coriolis force are the most influential factors in seawater circulation. Surface waters move in opposite directions on either side of the equator: Northern Hemisphere waters move eastward, and waters in the Southern Hemisphere tend to move westward. In a manner similar to that in which air circulates in the atmosphere, warm surface waters travel from regions near the equator toward the cooler poles, redistributing heat within the oceans. These wide, circular patterns are called gyres. When warm surface water reaches the higher latitudes, it is cooled by interaction with the ambient waters (and ice) and the air in the region. With the resulting increase in density, the water moves downward and cycles back toward the equator. Thus, gravity is the force that most affects deep-water circulation. Some of the water in this "oceanic conveyor belt" then rises back to the surface where it is warmed again and reenters the cycle. Other portions of water remain in the depths of the ocean.

Waves

There are two main processes in operation in the creation of wave motion: disturbing forces (such as wind, changes in atmospheric pressure, the mixing of water of different densities, and earthquakes) and restoring forces (the water's surface tension and gravity). In the creation of a wave, a disturbing force drives water into a pile, or crest. The water that makes up this crest comes from an adjacent section of water; therefore, the formation of the crest produces a depression, or trough, on a nearby water surface. Gravity, a restoring force, attempts to restore equilibrium by forcing the crest back down to sea level. Due to inertia, however, the gravitational force presses water down below that level, creating another trough. The water displaced by this motion forms another crest, which produces another trough, and the up and down motions continue. When the crest of a wave is higher than its associated trough, the wave moves forward. It is not the water that moves during wave motion, but the wave.

Wave length is defined as the horizontal distance between two equivalent wave phases (that is, the distance separating two sequential crests or troughs). The velocity of a wave is the distance it moves during a specified period of time. The period of a wave is the length of time required for two equivalent wave phases to pass a certain point. The number of periods that occur in a specified length of time is referred to as the frequency of the wave. These measurements vary greatly among waves. One of the largest such occurrences measured a wave length of 792 meters, a velocity of 126 kilometers per hour, and a period of 22.5 seconds.

Wave erosion

Most coastal erosion takes place when waves crash into a shore zone during a storm. It is at this time that the height of a wave (the distance between its upper effective limit and its lower effective limit, or wave base) is the greatest. The upper and lower limits of a wave work on a coastline much like a saw moving horizontally. Like river and stream erosion, most wave erosion is accomplished through abrasion caused by eroded materials (sand and gravel, for instance) carried in the water. Fluctuations in the tide cause coastal erosion indirectly—during low tide, large portions of the shore are exposed and vulnerable to other erosive agents, such as wind and rain. The energy of waves and the strength of the material of which a coastline is composed are the main factors in the rate of wave erosion.

Landforms created
The sea cliff is a landform that is often associated with coastal areas. Particularly large, high-energy waves attack coastlines during storms and abrade portions of a rock face, forming a usually steep cliff. The intensity of this effect is related to the durability of the material being eroded and the slope of the land surface. Wave erosion also produces wave-cut platforms, or a truncated sea cliff with a leveled surface. Sometimes these areas remain bare except for the irregularities created by the erosive process; these remnants of cliffs are called stacks. Beaches are created when the portion of the platform closest to the sea is covered with sand or other grainy materials. These formations are constantly being eroded away and reformed. A marine-built terrace (a deposit of material transported by waves) is often formed inland from a beach.

Stacks

Oceanic tides

Oceanic tides are the daily oscillations in sea level along coastlines. The number of times sea level changes and the differences in sea level vary with location, but all parts of the ocean experience this phenomenon. Tides occur due to the gravitational force and centripetal acceleration. Both the Sun and the Moon exert gravitational pulls on the Earth; however, the attraction of the Moon is more effective in tide formation, due to the fact that it is closer to our planet (because gravitational attraction varies with distance, among other things). As the Earth rotates, different areas of the oceans are closest to the Moon. Since water is not firmly affixed to the surface, it is disturbed by the Moon's gravitational pull, which creates an exceptionally long wave. Centripetal acceleration is the force that keeps the Earth and Moon in orbit around the Sun; this force is experienced equally at all points on the Earth's surface. The combined influence of these two forces produces the rhythmic pattern of oceanic tides.

Coastal upwelling

Coastal upwelling occurs due to the combined effects of wind and Ekman transport. Wind often blows parallel to a coastline; Ekman transport causes warm surface water along the shore to swing outward, away from land. Coastal upwelling happens when cooler water swells up from higher depths to replace the water moving away from the coast. The water that rises during coastal upwelling contains high levels of nutrients. Plants near the surface absorb these nutrients and consequently experience population growth. Fish and other marine organisms then come to the surface to feed on the plentiful vegetation. Thus, areas of coastal upwelling are some of the most fertile in the ocean.

Effects of ozone depletion on marine life

Ozone depletion affects marine life due to the harm caused by ultraviolet radiation. In the oceans, this electromagnetic energy can penetrate depths to 20 meters. This radiation can cause cell damage in marine species. Small organisms, such as plankton (plant and animal species), are especially susceptible to damage. When these organisms, which exist on the lowest tier of the food chain, are killed or mutated, effects radiate upward on the food chain. This process has the potential to decrease the global food supply. Ultraviolet radiation also affects fish, amphibians, shrimp, and other organisms in their developmental stages, decreasing their future reproductive capabilities. Again, this damage can move up the food chain and impact entire ecosystems.

Effects of pollution on oceans

Sewage, oil, garbage, and industrial waste are commonly disposed of in Earth's oceans. Also, the use of pesticides in agriculture can indirectly contribute to pollution—these chemicals are picked up by rainwater moving back to the oceans.

- 67 -

Ocean pollution has many harmful effects, both within oceanic ecosystems and across the rest of the globe. For example, pesticides deposited in the ocean contaminate the normally clean water in which algae thrive. When the algae die, a number of the fish that depend on algae (or other underwater plant life) for sustenance will die as well. This can affect local economies (not to mention food supplies) that depend on fishing. Also, when toxic waste is dumped into an ocean, it may be consumed by organisms low on the food chain. If it does not kill these organisms, they can be eaten by larger predators. Pollutants can continue to move up the food chain and eventually be consumed by humans. Lead, for instance, is commonly found in seafood eaten by humans.

Runoff, watershed, groundwater and infiltration

Runoff is precipitation that does not experience evaporation, transpiration by plants, or infiltration (the process in which water transitions from surface water to groundwater). It is an important part of the hydrologic cycle. Runoff, or surface water, moves from the location where it falls as precipitation across the surface of the Earth to an ocean. Rivers and streams are the mechanisms of transportation for surface water. Moving runoff often picks up soil and other materials as it travels. A watershed is the area in which runoff moves toward a body of water; such a region is usually bounded by hills and/or mountains. Groundwater is precipitation that seeps through the upper layers of the Earth's surface. This process of infiltration is also referred to as groundwater recharge. Water moves underground back to the oceans from where it came at the beginning of the hydrologic cycle. When the water reaches its destination, it is deposited through groundwater discharge.

Water table and saturated zone

The water table is the upper boundary of the region in which groundwater moves. It is the level at which water stands in wells. The water table is not level. Rather, it resembles the surface of the Earth, with depressions and elevated portions. This shelf intersects the Earth's surface at streams, springs, and lakes. Low-elevation streams that receive additional water from the water table are called effluent streams. This type of stream is common in humid areas. Influent streams are those that contribute water to the underground supply; they usually exist in arid regions at high elevations. The saturated zone is the area below the water table; it is so named because the pore space of the rocks in this zone is filled to capacity with water.

Movement of surface water to oceans

Precipitation that does not evaporate or seep into the Earth's surface may fall into a watershed, or it may be transported to one by gravity (if, for example, it falls on a hillside). Water that enters a watershed will eventually enter the area's associated body of water. This surface water may move directly to an ocean, or it may move into a transportation medium such as a river or stream (a smaller river); it may also move into a lake, where it will be temporarily stored. A river is a body of water with a detectable current (fluid motion). The velocity of moving water in a river depends largely on the gradient (downward slope); it is also influenced by the shape of the channel through which it moves, the texture of the inside surfaces of the channel, and the amount of sediment in the water.

Glaciers

A glacier is a large mass of ice formed by the physical transformation of snow under certain conditions; this ice mass must also exhibit evidence of movement. These ice sheets form only in climates in which some level of snow remains on the ground year-round; this necessitates high amounts of snowfall in the winter and low temperatures in the summer. If a glacier forms on a hill or mountain slope, the formative process may also be influenced by the orientation of said slope, in that the south side of a slope receives more sunlight than the north, and that one side may experience greater wind or precipitation levels than the other. Glaciers are created when snow (solid water) thaws and subsequently freezes again, becoming a granular type of ice called neve, or firn. Neve accumulates and eventually compacts due to the pressure of snow and ice above it, completing the transition to glacier over a long period of time. Glaciers move due to gravity and the force of their own weight.

Movement
The center of a glacier flows more quickly than the sides and bottom of the mass because of the friction between the glacier and the surface upon which it moves at the latter two locations. Usually, glacial movement occurs at velocities of 3 to 300 meters per year. Sometimes, however, the bottom of a glacier detaches from the rock floor and moves downward very rapidly (sometimes up to 6,000 meters per year). This type of movement, called a glacial surge, generally occurs in valley glaciers. Basal slip is the glacial movement that actually involves the bottom of a glacier sliding along the surface upon which it rests, usually because of melting at the glacier's base. Basal slip leaves polished and scratched ground surface behind; this can be observed after a glacier melts. A glacier is said to move through plastic flow when the pressure created by the weight of (brittle) upper layers causes the ice crystals in the lower part of a glacier to become plastic and flow.

Alpine glaciers
Alpine glaciers (one of the main categories of glacier) form on valley or mountain slopes with summits above the snow line. Gravity is the main proponent of their movement, which usually follows a predefined pathway. The movements of alpine glaciers erode the land over which they travel in two principal ways. Glacial abrasion consists of the wearing down of the ground under the base of the moving glacier. Glacial quarrying pries surface rocks out of their location and embeds them in the glacier; the deep crevasses that may be left behind by this type of erosion provide much of the information we know about the process. The erosive processes of alpine glaciers produce several different kinds of landforms: for example, cirques

- 69 -

(rounded, steep-walled recesses in valley walls), tarns (lakes that form due to uneven erosion), and fjords (deep valleys that are partially below sea level). Glaciers also deposit the materials they acquire along their paths in landforms called moraines. Moraines are named for their location of deposition (terminal, lateral, or medial).

Continental glaciers

Continental glaciers are one of the two general categories of glacier. This type of glacier consists of a large sheet of ice. This type of glacier was prominent during the ice ages, when such formations covered over twenty million square kilometers of land. Unlike alpine glaciers, continental glaciers move over any object in their way (rather than following the path of least resistance). Consequently, this kind of glacier tends to smooth out the land over which it travels, instead of sharpening irregularities, as the movement of alpine glaciers does. Icebergs are formed when portions of a continental glacier breaks off and drifts out to sea. A kettle is a landform produced by continental glacial erosion. It is a depression formed when till (debris deposited by ice) builds up around a stationary glacier, which becomes trapped and then melts. A drumlin is a small, round hill believed to be created under a moving glacier; these usually appear in groups. Eskers are long, thin depositions of stratified sediment.

drumlin *esker* *kettle*

Rock glacier

A rock glacier is a large, tongue-shaped mass of rock and ice that behaves much like a glacier formed completely of ice. It forms on a slope in a valley and travels slowly (about one meter per year) downward. These bodies form in geographical locations where an ice glacier could not—where warm temperatures in the summer cause much of the snow that piled up in the winter to melt. Though they have not been extensively studied, scientists believe that some rock glaciers are composed of rock particles cemented by ice and others are formed when rocky debris accumulates and becomes frozen into glacial surfaces. Rock glaciers form at high altitudes near eroding cliffs—the altitude allows for some snow to remain into the summertime, and nearby cliffs supply enough rocks to cover the small amount of snow that remains.

Ice age

An ice age is a period of time in which the Earth's climate is significantly colder, enabling the expansion of glaciers and ice sheets. Based on sedimentary deposits (including fossils) and moraine deposits of till left by glaciers, scientists have identified four major ice ages in Earth's past. The most recent of these began about 40 million years ago and intensified about 2.5 million years ago; there have been several expansions and recessions of ice sheets (glacial periods) since that time. Several different hypotheses have been advanced to explain periods of glaciation. Suggested terrestrial causes include the presence of high mountains and large land areas in polar positions. Suggested atmospheric causes include changes in the composition of Earth's atmosphere, specifically, variations in carbon dioxide levels (related to the greenhouse effect). Suggested astronomical causes include changes in the tilt of Earth's rotational axis, variations in Earth's orbit around the Sun, and changes in Earth's inclination to the plane of its orbit.

Changes in climate

From about 1900 to the 1940s, most of the glaciers in the Northern Hemisphere were retreating. The global climate during that period of time included a general increase in atmospheric temperatures and changes in annual temperatures and precipitation on Earth. These climatic shifts caused corresponding shifts in ocean currents (and thus populations of marine organisms) and migrations among groups of land animals. Sometime in the 1940s, the climate shifted and began growing generally cooler and wetter than during the preceding years. Consequently, many glaciers expanded or at least halted their recession during this time. This trend once again reversed in the 1970s, when it shifted to warming once again. There is significant debate over what conclusions ought to be drawn, with accusations being made on both sides of money influencing scientific opinion. Currently, a majority of scientists attribute the overall increase of global temperatures to manmade causes.

Coasts

Emergent coasts are those that are rising. Plate tectonics are one mechanism by which a portion of land can rise. Wave-cut platforms provide evidence of this occurrence. Also, Earth's crust may rebound when it is relieved of the pressure caused by an overlying glacier. A submerged coast is sinking. In other words, the sea level is rising relative to a submerged coast. This type of coast is usually found where the shoreline has become embayed (the sea extends inland, with fingers of the coast reaching into the ocean). Prior surface water erosion is usually a factor in the formation of a submerged coast. Consequently, wave erosions focus on the portions of land around the embayments, which become sea cliffs. Eventually, the fingers of land jutting into the sea will disappear completely, resulting in a relatively straight coastline. A plains coast is surrounded by barrier islands (narrow strips of sandy land separated by the coast by lagoons).

Aeration zone

The aeration, or vardose, zone is the area above the water table. This zone consists of three sublayers: the zone of soil moisture (the portion of the surface that becomes damp after precipitation), the intermediate zone (a transition zone through which water moves downward), and the tension-saturated zone, or capillary fringe (an area where water is held in thin branches between soil particles). Water actually moves upward from the water table into the capillary fringe. This is accomplished through capillary action, whereby a liquid is drawn upward into a narrow space. Capillary action occurs when adhesive intermolecular forces are stronger between the molecules of the liquid and the molecules of the solid that comprises the tube than they are between the molecules of the liquid alone.

Porosity and permeability

Porosity is a characteristic of rocks that has a large effect on the rate of transportation of groundwater. It is expressed as the percentage of a rock that is occupied by empty space (pores). The porosity of a rock is determined by several variables. For example, in sedimentary rocks, the amount of cementing material that infiltrated pore space during lithification is a factor that affects the rock's porosity. In igneous and metamorphic rocks, porosity is influenced by the frequency of joints in the material. The measurement of the ability of a rock to transmit water through it is referred to as its permeability. A rock's permeability is closely related to the size of the openings in a rock and the extent to which those openings are connected. One rock may have a higher porosity but a lower permeability than another rock.

Aquifer

An aquifer is a layer of rock or other material (such as sand or silt) through which groundwater travels laterally between points of deposition. An aquifer is confined when it is bounded from above by a layer of impermeable material. This type of aquifer can often be found below an unconfined aquifer, one that has the water table as its upward boundary. This kind of aquifer is usually close to surface level. An aquiclude (also referred to as an aquitard or aquifuge) is a layer of impermeable material. A layer may become an aquiclude when it becomes too saturated to accommodate any more liquid. Many aquifers are semi-confined, existing at a state between confined and unconfined.

aquiclude : impermeable

Meteorology

Earth's atmosphere

Earth's atmosphere is a mixture of molecules and particles that envelop the planet. Today, this gaseous conglomeration is approximately 78 percent nitrogen and 21 percent oxygen, with trace gases such as the greenhouse gas carbon dioxide and the noble gas argon making up the remaining one percent. The majority of these elements are concentrated in the lowest ten kilometers of the atmosphere. The atmosphere's lower boundary is the Earth's surface, while its hazy upper boundary is 10,000 kilometers above that. The atmosphere shields the planet's surface from harmful cosmic rays and absorbs much of the ultraviolet radiation beamed towards the planet from the sun. The motion of air within the atmosphere helps to regulate the Earth's temperature through convection and by allowing certain amounts of thermal energy in from, and out to, space.

Formation
According to the best available scientific knowledge, the Earth's atmosphere has evolved through two stages and is currently in its third. This third stage is the only one capable of sustaining life in organisms that need oxygen. The first atmosphere is believed to have been composed of helium, hydrogen, methane, and ammonia; these gases probably collected around the planetesimal of the newly-formed Earth over 4 billion years ago. However, the planet was still very hot. This heat, along with the currents of stellar winds, dissipated this primordial atmosphere. The second atmosphere was created about 3.5 billion years ago, just after the crust had solidified. Volcanic activity on the new planet released water vapor, carbon dioxide, sulfur oxide, and nitrogen from the mantle into the atmosphere in a process called outgassing. This atmosphere was called reducing or reductive because it contained little or no oxygen and high amounts of hydrogen. During this time, the greenhouse effect probably prevented the Earth from freezing.

[handwritten in margin: reduction gains electrons]

Earth's second atmosphere was composed largely of carbon dioxide and water vapor with some nitrogen and minute levels of oxygen. About 3.3 billion years ago, photosynthesizing cyanobacteria evolved, and their respiration processes released large levels of oxygen into the atmosphere. Also, as the Earth cooled, the atmosphere cooled, causing water molecules to condense and produce rain clouds. Over the next few billion years, massive amounts of water then filled the crevices left on Earth's crust after it cooled and condensed, forming oceans and other water bodies. The gases which made up the second atmosphere then began to dissolve in the oceans. Some of these gases, such as carbon dioxide and sulfur oxide, produce acids when they are dissolved in water; this process also contributed to the rising levels of oxygen in the atmosphere. During this period, oxygen levels were actually too high to support life on Earth. It was only after organisms evolved oxidative respiration that the levels of oxygen in the air became balanced. The third atmosphere, maintained through gravity, was the result.

Lower levels

Variations in temperature and air pressure throughout the atmosphere delineate the lower level of the atmosphere into several layers. The lowest three layers are the troposphere, the stratosphere, and the mesosphere. The troposphere covers the area from surface level to about 16 kilometers and is the densest level of the atmosphere, containing three-quarters of the body's total mass. Generally, temperatures in this region decrease with increased elevation. Most of the weather experienced on Earth occurs in the troposphere, when the convection of air due to the temperature variations and the presence of moisture cause clouds to form. The tropopause, a region of stable temperatures, is the boundary between the troposphere and the stratosphere, located at roughly 16 to 50 kilometers above the surface. In this region, temperatures increase with altitude due to the ozone layer at this level absorbing ultraviolet radiation from the sun. Unlike the troposphere, this layer is calm and virtually weather-free, which makes it ideal for airplane flight. The stratosphere is separated from the mesosphere by the stratopause.

Upper levels

The mesosphere is the layer of the atmosphere approximately 50 to 80 kilometers above the Earth's surface. Temperatures in the mesosphere drop with increases in altitude; this layer can be as cold as -100 degrees Celsius, making it the coldest layer in the atmosphere. This causes the formation of clouds of ice called noctilucent clouds. The mesosphere is the layer in which most of the meteors that enter the atmosphere burn up and break apart. The mesopause separates this layer from the thermosphere, the uppermost layer of the Earth's atmosphere, about 80 to 640 kilometers above the surface. Its name, which literally means "sphere of heat," testifies to the fact that it is the warmest layer of the atmosphere—temperatures at this level may reach up to 1000 degrees Celsius. This is because the thermosphere absorbs high levels of energy from the sun.

The Earth's thermosphere is subdivided into the ionosphere and the exosphere. The ionosphere, located approximately 80 to 550 kilometers above the surface, is made up of ionized nitrogen and oxygen atoms as well as free electrons. These composite materials justify its classification as a sub-layer. The ionization process occurs in the ionosphere due to the high levels of ultraviolet radiation and x-rays that enter the region. Due to its composition, this level produces the phenomena of aurorae and is a good conductor of electromagnetic radio waves. The exosphere is the outermost division of the Earth's atmosphere at about 550-10,000 kilometers above the surface. The upper boundary of this layer of thin air is uncertain and variable because it merges with space. Satellites orbit the Earth at this level. The low-density exosphere is composed mostly of hydrogen and helium.

Ozone layer

The Earth's **ozone layer** is the region of the stratosphere with a high concentration of ozone (a form of oxygen) particles. These molecules are formed through the process of photolysis, which occurs when ultraviolet light from the sun collides with oxygen molecules (O2) in the atmosphere. The ultraviolet radiation splits the oxygen atoms apart; when a free oxygen atom strikes an oxygen molecule, it combines with the molecule to create an ozone particle (O3). Ozone molecules may be broken down by interaction with nitrogen-, chlorine-, and hydrogen-containing compounds, or by thermal energy from the sun. Under normal conditions, these creative and destructive processes balance the levels of ozone in the stratosphere. The concentration of ozone molecules in the atmosphere absorbs ultraviolet radiation, thus preventing this harmful energy from reaching the Earth's surface. Ozone particles form in the region of the atmosphere over the equator, which receives the most direct sunlight. Atmospheric winds then disperse the particles throughout the rest of the stratosphere.

Transpiration

Transpiration is the mechanism by which water evaporates into the atmosphere from the leaves or stems of plants. Plants absorb water into their roots through osmosis. Then, as explained by cohesion-tension theory, water moves upward from the roots of a plant to its leaves. Some transpiration occurs directly through surface cells on the stem of a plant. More often, however, water escapes through pores in its leaves called stomates. Water droplets on the exterior surface of the leaves (usually on the bottom of the leaves) are consequently subjected to the process of evaporation. The process of transpiration enables photosynthesis, which in turn releases vital oxygen into Earth's atmosphere. Transpiration also has a cooling affect on the surface and air around the plant.

Precipitation

Precipitation is water that falls back to Earth's surface from the atmosphere. This water may be in the form of rain, which is water in the liquid form. Raindrops are formed in clouds due to the process of condensation. When the drops become too heavy to remain in the cloud (due to a decrease in their kinetic energy), gravity causes them to fall down toward Earth's surface. Extremely small raindrops are called drizzle. If the temperature of a layer of air through which rain passes on its way down is below the freezing point, the rain may take the form of sleet (partially frozen water). Precipitation may also fall in the form of snow, or water molecules sublimated into ice crystals. When clumps of snowflakes melt and refreeze, hail is formed. Hail may also be formed when liquid water accumulates on the surface of a snowflake and subsequently freezes.

Air mass

An air mass is a body of air that exhibits consistent temperatures and levels of moisture throughout. These (usually large) pockets of air tend to come together under relatively still conditions, where air can remain in one place long enough to adopt the temperature and moisture characteristics of the land below it; this often occurs above wide areas of flat land. The region in which an air mass originates and the course of its motion are used to name it. For example, a maritime tropical air mass (denoted mT) is formed over the Gulf of Mexico (a tropical climate) and moves across the Atlantic Ocean (a maritime area). The conditions of an air mass will remain constant as long as the body is still, but when it moves across surfaces with different conditions, it may adopt those qualities. For example, polar air that moves over tropical land areas will be heated by the conditions below. Generally, maritime air masses contain high levels of moisture, and continental air masses are drier.

Meteorological depression

A meteorological depression refers to a low-pressure zone (created by rising air) situated between 30 and 60 degrees latitude. These zones vary from approximately 321-3,218 kilometers in diameter. The rising air associated with a depression usually condenses at higher levels in the atmosphere and causes precipitation. Depressions are formed when warm air masses and cold air masses converge. At first, a single front (boundary between converging masses of air with different temperatures) separates the air masses.

A distortion similar to the crest of a water wave develops, creating a small center of low pressure. Then, differentiated warm and cold fronts develop from that center. A mass of warm air forms and rises over the body of cold air. The cold front and the cold air eventually catch up with the warm air, creating an occluded front and causing pressure to rise, effectually slowing the depression's movement. Depressions usually have life spans of four to seven days.

Prevailing winds and wind belts

Wind (the horizontal movement of air with respect to Earth's surface) forms due to pressure gradients (differences) in the atmosphere. Air tends to move from areas of high pressure (such as the poles) to areas of low pressure (such as the tropics). Prevailing winds, or trade winds, are the winds (named in meteorology for the direction they come from) that blow most frequently in a particular region. For instance, the prevailing winds most common in the region from 90 to 60 degrees north latitude blow from the northeast, and are generally called the Polar Easterlies. Wind belts are created in areas where prevailing winds converge with other prevailing winds or air masses. The Inter-Tropical Convergence Zone (ITCZ), where air coming from tropical areas north and south of the equator come together, is an example of a wind belt.

Coriolis force

The Coriolis force, which gives rise to the Coriolis effect, is not really a force at all. Rather, it appears to be there to us because the Earth is a rotating frame of reference and we are inside it. In the atmosphere, air tends to move from areas of high pressure to areas of lower pressure. This air would move in a straight line but for the Coriolis force, which appears to deflect the air and cause it to swirl. Really, however, the Earth moves underneath the wind, which creates the impression of swirling air to someone standing on the Earth's surface. The Coriolis force causes winds to swing to the right as they approach the Northern Hemisphere and to the left as they approach the Southern Hemisphere.

Air stability in the atmosphere

Air stability is the tendency for air to rise or fall through the atmosphere under its own power. Heated air rises because it is less dense than the surrounding air. As a pocket of air rises, however, it will expand and become cooler with changes in atmospheric pressure. If the ambient air into which rising air ascends does not cool as quickly with altitude as the rising air does, that air will rapidly become cooler (and heavier) than the surrounding air and descend back to its original position. The air in this situation is said to be stable. However, if the air into which the warm pocket rises becomes colder with increased altitude, the warm air will continue its ascent. In this case, the air is unstable. Unstable air conditions (such as those that exist in depressions) lead to the formation of large clouds of precipitation.

Clouds

The four main types of clouds are cirrus, cumulous, nimbus, and stratus. A cirrus cloud forms high in a stable atmosphere, generally at altitudes of 6,000 meters or higher. Temperatures at these altitudes (in the troposphere) decrease with increased altitude; therefore, the precipitation in a cirrus cloud adopts the form of ice crystals. These usually thin traces of clouds may indicate an approaching weather depression. A cumulous cloud is a stereotypical white, fluffy ball. Cumulous clouds are indicators of a stable atmosphere, and also of the vertical extent of convection in the atmosphere—condensation and cloud formation begin at the flat base of a cumulous cloud. The more humid the air, the lower a cumulous cloud will form. A nimbus cloud is, generally speaking, a rain cloud. Nimbus clouds are usually low, dark, and formless, sometimes spanning the entire visible sky. A stratus cloud is basically a cloud of fog which forms at a distance above the Earth's surface. This type of cloud forms when weak convective currents bring moisture just high enough to initiate condensation (if the temperature is below the dew point).

The four cloud subtypes are cumulonimbus, cirrostratus, altocumulus, and stratocumulus. A cumulonimbus cloud is produced by rapid convection in unstable air. This type of cloud (which is often dark) is formed as a large, tall "tower."

- 77 -

Collections of these towers (squall lines) often signal a coming cold front. Thunderstorms often involve cumulonimbus clouds. A cirrostratus cloud is an ultra-thin formation with a white tint and a transparent quality. An altocumulus cloud forms at an altitude from 1,980 to 6,100 meters. Clouds of this type, which appear to be flattened spheres, often form in clumps, waves, or lines. A stratocumulus cloud forms as a globular mass or flake. Stratocumulus clouds usually come together in layers or clumps.

alto cumulus (handwritten)

Climate

Climate is usually defined as the "average weather" in a particular area on Earth. The timespan over which climate is measured is variable, but it is generally accepted that the climate of an area does not vary during a human life span (though climate is extremely various in geologic time). This may change, however, due to the increasing greenhouse effect. Meteorologists measure climate by averaging certain quantifiable elements such as rainfall or temperature. Climate may be studied on several different scales:

- Local climate refers to the climate of small geographic areas (generally up to tens of miles wide). The local climate of an area is affected by things such as its location relative to an ocean and the presence of mountains near the location.
- A regional climate is the climate of a larger geographic area, such as a country. A regional climate may also be delineated due to climate features that are distinctive from the surrounding climate.
- Global climate refers to the average weather experienced across the Earth.

Climate zones
Climate zones are areas of regional climate. These zones are created by the general circulation of the air in Earth's atmosphere. Generally, the warmest air moves from the equator (where the greatest amount of solar energy is received) toward the higher latitudes at the poles. The latitudinal temperature gradient produces atmospheric pressure. At the equator, solar energy heats air near the surface, causing it to rise and decreasing air pressure. The risen air is transported by winds to cooler areas at higher latitudes, where the air then descends (because cool air is heavier than warmer air), creating an area of high pressure. The descended air is then moved by surface winds, either back to the equator or up to higher latitudes, where it encounters colder air. The air then rises again in an area of low pressure. The air in polar regions is very cold, which causes it to sink, creating high pressure. Winds are thus generated to move air from warmer regions to colder ones.

desc high pre warm (handwritten marginalia)

Tropical, subtropical, and polar climate zones
The tropical (low-latitude) climate zone covers the area around the equator. This area receives a large portion of the sun's solar energy, making average temperatures in this zone fairly high. The consistent levels of hot air in the region indicate that air is often moving upward. This convective process, in turn, produces large levels of

precipitation in the area, resulting in a humid climate. Seasons in the tropical zone are delineated by the amount of rainfall, instead of by changes in temperatures.

Subtropical (mid-latitude) climate zones are found about thirty degrees north and south of the equator. These zones generally consist of dry descending air, clear skies, and high atmospheric pressure. Desert climates (extreme heat during the day, cold temperatures at night, and lack of precipitation) are common in these zones.

Polar (high-latitude) climate zones are found at the north and south poles. They are characterized by high air pressure (due to descending air), low temperatures (rarely above freezing), and lack of precipitation (because air cannot evaporate from frozen water).

Maritime, continental, and temperate climates

Maritime climates are greatly affected by airflow from nearby oceans. This influence prevents extreme temperatures in such regions, which normally experience cool summers and mild winters. Also, maritime climates are usually quite humid, with large amounts of precipitation. Continental climates, unlike maritime climates, experience variations in temperature with changes in seasons, i.e., cold winters and hot summers. This is so because rock and soil have lower heat capacities than water, which serves to moderate ambient temperatures. Continental climates are usually relatively dry. A temperate climate is one with low variation in average temperature. Temperate climates may be maritime or continental.

Interactions between atmosphere and hydrosphere

The hydrosphere (all the water on Earth), specifically the oceans, stores much higher quantities of heat energy than the atmosphere is able to hold. Energy in the oceans, like energy in the atmosphere, is transferred around the globe, redistributing heat from areas of low latitudes to areas of high latitudes. Water on the surface of the ocean is driven by atmospheric wind patterns. Energy transfers between the oceans and the atmosphere affect temperatures and precipitation in regions across the globe. For example, the Gulf Stream is an ocean current that exerts an important influence on the climates of the United Kingdom and northwest Europe. This surface current originates in the Gulf of Mexico and carries warm water (about 25 degrees Celsius) northeast across the Atlantic at speeds of three miles per hour. When the ocean cools down at night, it releases warm air, regulating the temperatures of the regions mentioned above. Without the activity of the Gulf Stream, those regions would be as cold as Canada (which is at roughly the same latitude).

Warm

Milankovic cycles

The phenomenon of Milankovic cycles has been advanced as an explanation of the periodic ice ages experienced on Earth. Variations in the Earth's orbit (including precession, the wobble of the rotational axis, and eccentricities, or variations, in the shape of the orbit path) due to the gravitational attraction between our planet and other celestial bodies affect the amount of solar energy received at different locations on Earth's surface. In the long term, these variations lead to climate changes that, in turn, can cause Earth to enter an ice age. For example, if the Northern Hemisphere receives decreasing amounts of direct sunlight, temperatures will drop. This can cause increased levels of snow buildup, which reflects solar energy, increasing the possibility of glaciation. Milankovic believed that when all of Earth's orbital variations happened to line up and reinforce one another, the climate change could be severe enough to cause an ice age.

Lightning

Lightning is a natural electrostatic discharge that produces light and releases electromagnetic radiation. It is believed that the separation of positive and negative charge carriers within a cloud is achieved by the polarization mechanism. The first step of this mechanism occurs when falling precipitation particles become electrically polarized after they move through the Earth's magnetic field. The second step of the polarization mechanism involves electrostatic induction, the process whereby electrically charged particles create charges in other particles without direct contact. Ice particles are charged though this method, and then energy-storing electric fields are formed between the charged particles. The positively-charged ice crystals tend to rise to the top of the cloud, effectively polarizing the cloud with positive charges on top and negative charges at the middle and bottom. When charged clouds conglomerate, an electric discharge (a lightning bolt) is produced, either between clouds or between a cloud and the Earth's surface.

Thunderstorms

A thunderstorm is a weather phenomenon that includes lightning, thunder, and usually large amounts of precipitation and strong winds. Thunder is the noise made by the rapid expansion and contraction of air due to the heat energy produced by lightning bolts. A thunderstorm develops when heating on the Earth's surface causes large amounts of air to rise into an unstable atmosphere. This results in large clouds of rain and ice crystals. The associated condensation releases high levels of heat, which in turn power the growth cycle of the cloud. The clouds created during thunderstorms are immense, sometimes reaching widths of several miles and extending to heights of 10,000 meters or more. The precipitation in such clouds eventually becomes heavy enough to fall against the updraft of unstable air; the consequent downpour is often short but intense. The differential speeds at which light and sound travel through the atmosphere enable one to estimate the distance between oneself and the storm by observing the interval between a lightning bolt and a thunderclap.

Hurricanes

Hurricanes form when several conditions are met: Oceanic water must be at least 26 degrees Celsius, the general circulation pattern of wind must be disrupted (this disruption usually takes the form of an atmospheric wave in the easterly trade winds), and the Coriolis force must be in effect. During hurricane season (June to November), easterly waves appear in the trade winds every few days. When such a wave occurs over a body of particularly warm, deep water, it is strengthened by the evaporation of warm air from below. Surrounding winds converge at the low-pressure zone created by the wave; air brought by these winds rises because it has nowhere else to go. The large body of warm, moist air rises high into the atmosphere and consequently condenses into huge clouds. As more and more humid air is drawn upward, this air begins to rotate around the area of low pressure. The storm continues to gain strength and may move toward land.

El Nino

El Niño refers to the unusual warming of surface waters near the equatorial coast of South America. This phenomenon occurs during the winter approximately every two to seven years, lasting from a few weeks to a few months. El Nino can cause torrential rains, violent winds, drought, and dangerously high temperatures in surrounding areas. El Nino is caused by a reversal of the atmospheric pressures on the eastern and western sides of the Pacific (normally, pressure is high on the eastern side near South America and lower on the western side near the Indonesian coast). This reversal causes a wave of warm water to flow eastward and sea levels to fall on the western side. The changes in air pressure and ocean temperature cause moisture levels in the western Pacific to rise drastically while the region east of the Pacific experiences drought. The air pressure changes also weaken the region's trade winds, which normally serve to distribute heat and moisture.

Monsoons and savannahs

The term monsoon refers to a unique pattern of moving air and currents that occurs when winds reverse direction with a change in season. India and Southeast Asia experience the most intense monsoons. This area lies between tropical and subtropical climate zones. During the winter season, northeasterly winds (which are generally dry) move from high-pressure subtropical areas to lower-pressure tropical areas. During the summer season, the continents of India and Asia heat up, creating a low-pressure zone. This causes winds to reverse and blow southwesterly across the Indian Ocean, accumulating high levels of moisture, thereby creating large amounts of precipitation during this season.

Savannahs also exist between wet equatorial and dry subtropical climate zones. These regions are characterized by vegetation consisting mainly of shrubs and grass. Savannahs experience dry weather throughout most of the year. A single, brief rainy season that occurs when the Sun is directly above the region interrupts prolonged dry spells.

Influence of mountains on climate

At the level of local climate, the presence of mountains forces air to rise to travel above them; this contributes to increased formation of clouds and consequently, increases in levels of precipitation. Mountain chains can affect regional and even global climates by deflecting airflow. The Coriolis force causes most of Earth's atmospheric airflow to move east and west. Therefore, the presence of north–south–oriented mountain chains can alter general circulation patterns. For example, the Rocky Mountains force air to move northward; the air cools near the North Pole before blowing back down. This causes winter temperatures in Canada and parts of the United States to be very cold.

Weather

Weather is the result of transfers of kinetic (heat) energy due to differences in temperature between objects as well as transfers of moisture in Earth's atmosphere. Meteorology, the study of weather, covers the same natural events as climatology, but observes them on a shorter time scale (usually no more than a few days). Rain, fog, snow, and wind are all examples of weather phenomena. The processes that occur at different stages in the hydrologic cycle form the basis of meteorological events. Most of the activity that produces the weather we experience on Earth takes place in the troposphere, the lowest level of the atmosphere. Atmospheric pressure, temperature, humidity, elevation, wind speed, and cloud cover are all factors in the study of weather.

Humidity and cloud cover

Humidity is a measure of the amount of water vapor in the air. Specific humidity is the expression of humidity as a ratio of aqueous vapor to dry air; it is expressed as a ratio of mass of water vapor per unit mass of natural (dry) air. Absolute humidity measures the mass of water vapor in a given volume of moist air or gas; it is expressed in grams per cubic foot or per cubic meter. The equilibrium (or saturated) vapor pressure of a gas is the vapor pressure (created by the movement of molecules) of water vapor when air is saturated with water vapor. Relative humidity, usually expressed as a percentage, is the ratio of the vapor pressure of water in air (or another gas) to the equilibrium vapor pressure. In other words, it is a ratio of the mass of water per volume of gas and the mass per volume of a saturated gas. Cloud cover refers to the amount of sky blocked by clouds at a given location.

Measuring weather

Weather can be measured by a variety of methods. The simplest include measurement of rainfall, sunshine, pressure, humidity, temperature, and cloudiness with basic instruments such as thermometers, barometers, and rain gauges. However, the use of radar (which involves analysis of microwaves reflecting off of raindrops) and satellite imagery grants meteorologists a look at the big picture of weather across, for example, an entire continent. This helps them understand and make predictions about current and developing weather systems. Infrared (heat-sensing) imaging allows meteorologists to measure the temperature of clouds above ground. Using weather reports gathered from different weather stations spread over an area, meteorologists create synoptic charts. The locations and weather reports of several stations are plotted on a chart; analysis of the pressures reported from each location, as well as rainfall, cloud cover, and so on, can reveal basic weather patterns.

Global warming

The natural greenhouse effect of the atmosphere is beneficial to life on Earth; it keeps temperatures on the planet 33 degrees higher than they would be without this phenomenon. Originally, this helped sustain life. However, it has been discovered in the last 20 years that this effect is being intensified by the actions of humans. In the twentieth century, certain activities of mankind, including the burning of fossils fuels like coal and oil, have resulted in an increase in the levels of greenhouse gases (such as methane and carbon dioxide) being released into the atmosphere. Also, increasing deforestation has affected the number of photosynthesis-practicing plants. The combined effect of these trends is a higher-than-normal concentration of greenhouse gases in the atmosphere. This, in turn, produces the effect of global warming. The average temperature at the Earth's surface has gone up 0.6 degrees Celsius in the last 100 years. Continuation of this trend is likely to have a detrimental effect on many of the planet's ecosystems, including that of human beings.

Ozone depletion

Ozone depletion occurs when the balance between creation and destruction of ozone particles in the stratosphere is tipped toward destruction. Chlorofluorocarbons (or CFCs) are chemicals created by humans for use in, for example, refrigeration, aerosol cans, and cleaners. When these chemicals interact with sunlight in the atmosphere, chlorine atoms are released; these free atoms participate in processes that destroy ozone particles. An ozone hole (an area of severe ozone depletion) has been identified over Antarctica, where spring sunlight contributes to the chlorine-ozone reactions that destroy the latter molecule.

Important terms

Dip - Dip is the angle that a rock body or structural rock surface makes with the horizontal surface plane. True dip is quantified through downward measurement of the angle in the direction of greatest inclination; apparent dip is the measurement of dip in any direction. Dip is equal to zero in the direction of strike and has its maximum measurement in the direction of true dip.

Fracture zone - A fracture zone is an area surrounding a transform fault, created by inconsistent rates of seafloor spreading.

Graben: A graben is a depressed portion of land between two parallel, normal geologic faults.

Horst - A horst is a raised portion of land (a ridge) between two parallel, normal faults.

Hot spot - A hot spot is an area of the Earth's surface that experiences high levels of volcanic activity, created by hypothetical phenomena called mantle plumes. Mantle plumes are exceptionally hot portions of the Earth's mantle that rise (through convection) to the crust. Hot spots are responsible for the formation of volcanic chains such as the Hawaiian Islands.

Intensity - Intensity is a measure of the effects of an earthquake on a particular area and its human inhabitants. This measurement is more subjective, and thus less scientifically reliable, than the measurement of magnitude because measurement is usually taken in the area with the most damage and can be affected by localized factors such as building design. The intensity of earthquakes is measured on the Mercalli (or Modified Mercalli) scale in the United States and on the European Macroseismic Scale in the European Union.

Ionosphere - The ionosphere is the inner layer of Earth's magnetosphere. Consisting of a plasma made up of nitrogen and oxygen ionized by X-rays and ultraviolet radiation from the Sun, the Earth's ionosphere enables the use of radio waves for communication around the globe.

Magnitude - Magnitude refers to the strength of an earthquake, and it is observed qualitatively through measurement of the strain energy released during such an event. Charles Richter formulated a scale to describe relative magnitudes of earthquakes based on a progression of logarithmic values of magnitude.

Plastic deformation - Plastic, or ductile, deformation is permanent deformation—a material cannot recover after the introduction and subsequent removal of a load.

Proportional elastic limit - The proportional elastic limit of a substance is the maximum level of stress that a material can endure and still be able to recover to its original shape with the release of stress.

Rupture strength - Rupture strength refers to the amount of stress a material can withstand (for a period of time, at a certain temperature) before it ruptures. Ultimate strength - Ultimate strength is the greatest level of stress a material can endure before or during rupture; this can be tensional strength (resistance to lengthwise deformation), compressional strength (resistance to rupture under compression), or shear strength (resistance to a tangential force).

Tension   Compression   Shear

- 84 -

Slip - Slip is a measurement of the net relative displacement of structural surfaces along a fault.

Solar variation - Solar variation refers to changes in the amount of energy emitted by the Sun. Higher levels of solar radiation can contribute to the visual phenomena of polar aura (caused by interaction between Earth's magnetosphere, magnetic field, and atmosphere and a solar wind).

Solar wind - Solar winds are made up of hydrogen and helium ions (protons and electrons) in the form of plasma. These particles are able to escape the Sun's surface due to their high levels of thermal energy. They flow through space like a wind. This solar wind is deflected around the Earth by the magnetosphere like air around the nose of a jet.

Strike - Strike is the direction of a line of intersection drawn between the horizontal surface plane and the surface of an uptilted rock structure.

Subsidence - Subsidence is the downward motion of the Earth's crust. This process occurs when the lithosphere is stretched and cracked, and hot portions of the asthenosphere rise to fill the resultant void. Consequently, the crust and upper mantle heat up. This heat energy is later released from the surface as radiation; the lithosphere then cools and contracts.

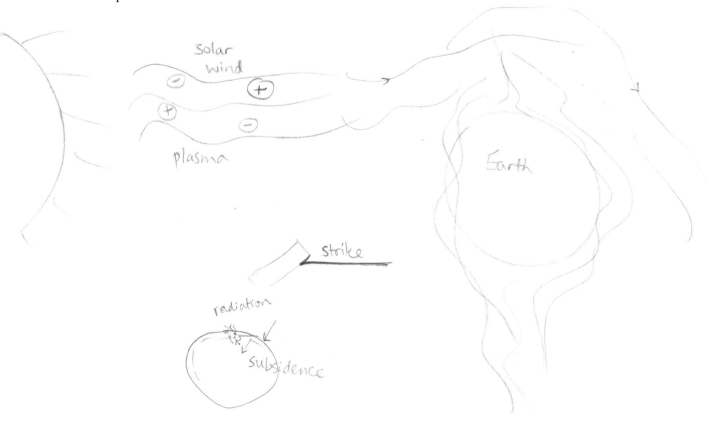

Astronomy

Earth's rotation

The Earth rotates west to east about its axis, an imaginary straight line that runs nearly vertically through the center of the planet. This rotation (which takes 23 hours, 56 minutes, and 5 seconds) places each section of the Earth's surface in a position facing the Sun for a period of time, thus creating the alternating periods of light and darkness we experience as day and night. This rotation constitutes a sidereal day; it is measured as the amount of time required for a reference star to cross the meridian (an imaginary north-south line above an observer). Each star crosses the meridian once every (sidereal) day. Since the speed at which Earth rotates is not exactly constant, we use the mean solar day (a 24-hour period) in timekeeping rather than the slightly variable sidereal day.

Sun

The Sun is the vital force of life on Earth; it is also the central component of our solar system. It is basically a sphere of extremely hot gases (close to 15 million degrees at the core) held together by gravity. Some of these gaseous molecules are ionized due to the high temperatures. The balance between its gravitational force and the pressure produced by the hot gases is called hydrostatic equilibrium. The source of the solar energy that keeps the Sun alive and plays a key role in the perpetuation of life on Earth is located in the Sun's core, where nucleosynthesis produces heat energy and photons. The Sun's atmosphere consists of the photosphere, the surface visible from Earth, the chronosphere, a layer outside of and hotter than the photosphere, the transition zone (the region where temperatures rise between the chronosphere and the corona), and the corona, which is best viewed at X-ray wavelengths. A solar flare is an explosive emission of ionized particles from the Sun's surface.

Earth's revolution around the Sun

Like all celestial objects in our solar system, planet Earth revolves around the Sun. This process takes approximately 365 1/4 days, the period of time that constitutes a calendar year. The path of the orbit of Earth around the Sun is not circular but elliptical. Therefore, the distances between the Earth and the Sun at points on either extreme of this counterclockwise orbit are not equal. In other words, the distance between the two objects varies over the course of a year. At perihelion, the minimum heliocentric distance, Earth is 147 million kilometers from the Sun. At aphelion, the maximum heliocentric distance, Earth is 152 million kilometers from the Sun. This movement of the Earth is responsible for the apparent annual motions of the Sun (in a path referred to as the ecliptic) and other celestial objects visible from Earth's surface.

Seasons

The combined effects of Earth's revolution around the Sun and the tilt of the planet's rotational axis create the seasons. Earth's axis is not perfectly perpendicular to its orbital plane; rather, it is tilted about 23.5 degrees. Thus, at different times of the year, certain areas of the surface receive different amounts of sunlight. For example, during the period of time in Earth's orbit when the Northern Hemisphere is tipped toward the Sun, it is exposed to higher amounts of nearly direct sunlight than at any other time of year (days are longer, and the direction of Sun's rays striking the surface is nearly perpendicular). This period of time is summer in the Northern Hemisphere and winter in the Southern Hemisphere; on the opposite side of the orbit, the seasons are reversed in each hemisphere.

Summer and winter solstices
The summer solstice occurs when Earth's orbital position and axial tilt point the North Pole most directly toward the Sun. This happens on or near June 21 each year. On this day in the Northern Hemisphere, the Sun appears to be directly overhead (at its zenith) at 12:00 noon. The entire Arctic Circle (the north polar region above approximately 66.5 degrees north latitude) is bathed in sunlight for a complete solar day. The North Pole itself experiences constant daylight for six full months. Conversely, the winter solstice occurs when the South Pole is oriented most directly toward the Sun. This phenomenon, which falls on or near December 22 each year, orients the Sun as viewed from the Northern Hemisphere at its lowest point above the horizon.

Equinoxes
The ecliptic (the Sun's apparent path through the sky) crosses Earth's equatorial plane twice during the year; these intersections occur when the North Pole is at a right angle from the line connecting the Earth and the Sun. At these times, the two hemispheres experience equal periods of light and dark. These two points in time are respectively referred to as the vernal (spring) equinox (on or about March 21) and the autumnal (fall) equinox (on or about September 23). A calendar year is measured as the length of time between vernal equinoxes.

Moon

Earth's Moon is historically one of the most studied celestial bodies. Its mass is approximately 1.2% of the Earth's mass, and its radius is just over one-fourth of the size of the Earth's radius. Measurements of the Moon's density suggest that its characteristics are similar to those of the rocks that make up Earth's crust. The landscape of the Moon consists mostly of mountains and craters formed by collisions of this surface with meteors and other interplanetary materials. The Moon's crust (estimated to be 50 to 100 kilometers in thickness) is made up of a layer of regolith (lunar soil) supported by a layer of loose rocks and gravel. Beneath the crust is a mantle made up of a solid lithosphere and a semiliquid asthenosphere.

The Moon's core (the innermost 500 kilometers of the body) is not as dense as that of the Earth. The Moon is made up mostly of refractory elements with high melting and boiling points with low levels of heavy elements such as iron.

Formation theories
The fission model of Moon origin suggests that the Moon is actually a piece of the Earth that split off early during the planet's formation. In this model, a portion of the Earth's mantle fissioned off during a liquid stage in its formation, creating the Moon. According to the capture model, the Moon formed elsewhere in the solar system and was subsequently captured by the Earth's gravitational field. The double-impact model states that the Earth and the Moon formed during the same period of time from the same accretion material. Each of these theories has its strengths, but none of them can explain all of the properties of the Moon and its relationship to the Earth. Recently, a fourth (widely accepted) hypothesis has been suggested, which involves the collision between the Earth and a large asteroid. This hypothetical collision is said to have released a large amount of Earth's crustal material into its orbit; the Moon accreted from that material and the material displaced from the asteroid due to the collision.

Earth-Moon system
While the Moon is commonly referred to as a satellite of the Earth, this is not entirely accurate. The ratio of the masses of the two bodies is much larger than that of any other planet-satellite system. Also, the Moon does not truly revolve around the Earth. Rather, the two bodies revolve around a common center of mass beneath the surface of the Earth (approximately 4,800 kilometers from Earth's core). The orbital planes of the Moon and the Earth are nearly aligned; therefore, the Moon moves close to the ecliptic, as seen from Earth. Due to the Moon's synchronous rotation (its rotation period and orbital period are equal); the same side of the Moon is always facing Earth. This occurs because of the mutual gravitational pull between the two bodies.

Phases
The sidereal period of the Moon (the time it takes the Moon to orbit the Earth with the fixed stars as reference points) is about 27 days. The lunar month (or synodic period) is the period of time required for the Moon to return to a given alignment as observed from the Earth with the Sun as a reference point; this takes 29 days, 12 hours, 44 minutes, and 28 seconds. A discrepancy exists between the two periods of time because the Earth and the Moon move at the same time. Sunlight reflected off of the Moon's surface at different times during the lunar month causes its apparent shape to change. The sequence of the Moon's shapes is referred to as the phases of the Moon. The full Moon can be viewed when the body is directly opposite from the Sun. The opposite end of the cycle, the new Moon, occurs when the Moon is not visible from Earth because it is situated between the Earth and the Sun.

<u>Configurations</u>
The configurations of the Moon describe its position with respect to the Earth and the Sun. We can thus observe a correlation between the phases of the Moon and its configuration. The Moon is at conjunction at the time of the new Moon—it is situated in the same direction as the Sun. Quadrature (which signals the first quarter phase) is the position of the Moon at a right angle between the Earth-Sun line; we see exactly half of the Moon's sunlit hemisphere. This is the waxing crescent phase, in which we see more of the Moon each night. Then comes opposition (which occurs when the Moon lies in the direction opposite the Sun)—we see the full Moon. After this point, the Moon enters its waning gibbons phase as it travels back toward quadrature. When it reaches that point again, it has entered the third-quarter phase. Finally, as the Moon circles back toward conjunction, it is in its waning crescent phase.

Terrestrial planets

The term terrestrial planets refers to the four planets closest to the Sun (Mercury, Venus, Earth, and Mars). They are classified together because they share many similarities that distinguish them from the giant planets. The terrestrial planets have high densities and atmospheres that constitute a small percentage of their total masses. These atmospheres consist mostly of heavy elements, such as carbon dioxide, nitrogen, and water, and are maintained by the gravitational field of the planets (which could not prevent hydrogen from escaping). These planets exhibit magnetic fields of varying intensity. An important characteristic that distinguishes the terrestrial planets from the giant planets is the evidence of various levels of internally generated activity, which caused these planets to evolve from their original states. These processes are thought to have been caused by constant meteoritic impacts during the first few hundred million years of the planets' existence. Radioactive decay of certain isotopes increased the internal temperatures of these planets, leading to volcanic activity on all of the terrestrial planets except Venus.

<u>Mercury</u>
Mercury, the smallest interior planet, is the least well known of the four. This is due to its close proximity to the Sun and high temperatures. Mercury's atmosphere is not very dense; this means that the planet's surface experiences wide temperature differentials from day to night. Mercury's density is close to that of Earth. As the smallest planet known to have experienced planetary evolution, Mercury's internal activity ceased (it became extinct) thousands of millions of years ago. The size of the planet is relevant because less massive bodies cool more quickly than larger ones after cessation of radioactivity. Mercury's surface is characterized by craters produced by meteoritic impact.

<u>Venus</u>
Venus is comparable to Earth in both mass and density. Venus is the brightest planet in the sky (partially due to the fact that it is proximate to the Sun), which makes

exploration of its surface difficult. This planet's atmosphere consists mainly of carbon dioxide, with trace amounts of water and carbon oxide molecules, as well as high levels of sulfuric, nitric, and hydrofluoric acids in the clouds that characterize this atmosphere. The concentration of clouds, coupled with the chemical makeup of Venus's atmosphere, result in a strong greenhouse effect at the planet's surface. This surface consists of large plains (thought to be created by either volcanic activity, which remains unproven, or by meteoritic impacts) and large impact craters. The materials that compose Venus's surface are highly radioactive. Some astronomers have suggested past single-plate tectonic activity; again, however, the planet's dense atmosphere makes valid surface observation quite difficult.

Mars

Mars and Earth exhibit many similarities. For example, Mars has an internal structure that includes a central metallic core, a mantle rich in olivine and iron oxide, and a crust of hydrated silicates. Martian soil consists largely of basalts and clay silicate, with elements of sulfur, silicon oxide, and iron oxide. The planet's surface belies high levels of past volcanic activity (though, due to its relatively small mass, it is probably extinct). In fact, Mars is home to the largest known volcano in the solar system. The Martian landscape also includes two major basins, ridges and plateaus, and, most notably, apparent evidence of fluvial (water-based) erosion landforms, such as canyons and canals. It is possible that the past pressures and temperatures on Mars allowed water to exist on the red planet. Some have gone so far as to suggest that this planet was a site of biochemical evolution. So far, however, no evidence of life has been found.

Mars's satellites: Two Martian satellites have been observed: Phobos and Deimos. Each of these bodies is ellipsoidal; the circular orbits of the two satellites lie in Mars's equatorial plane. The gravitational forces between this planet and Phobos and Deimos have caused both satellites to settle into synchronous rotation (the same parts of their surfaces are always facing Mars). This feature exerts a braking force on Phobos's orbit. In other words, its orbit is decreasing in size. The relationship between Deimos and Mars is similar to the Earth-Moon system, in which the radius of the satellite's orbit is gradually growing. The differential compositions and densities of Mars and its satellites indicate that Phobos and Deimos probably did not break off from Mars.

Giant planets

The large diameters of Jupiter, Saturn, Uranus, and Neptune gave rise to the name of the category into which they fall. The hypothetical icy cores of these planets cause them to exhibit primary atmospheres, because the large levels of mass they accreted prevented even the lightest elements from escaping their gravitational pulls. The atmospheres of the giant planets thus consist mostly of hydrogen and helium. The giant planets do not have solid surfaces like those of the terrestrial planets. Jupiter probably consists of a core (made of ice and rock) surrounded by a layer of metallic hydrogen, which is covered by a convective atmosphere of hydrogen and helium.

Saturn is believed to have the same type of core and hydrogen mantle, enriched by the helium missing from the atmosphere, surrounded by a differentiation zone and a hydrogenic atmosphere. Uranus and Neptune probably have the same type of core, surrounded by ionic materials, bounded by methane-rich molecular envelopes. Uranus is the only giant planet that exhibits no evidence of internal activity.

Rings

Each of the four giant planets exhibits rings. These are flat disks of fragmented material that orbit just next to their respective planets. Many of the giant planets' smaller satellites are embedded in these rings. There are two main hypotheses regarding the formation of such rings. One theory suggests that the tidal force exerted on a satellite by its planet may surpass the Roche limit (the point at which particle cohesion is no longer possible) and break the satellite into fragments, which then collide and become smaller. This material then spreads out and forms a ring. An alternate theory of the formation of the rings of the giant planets suggests that there was unaccreted material left over after the formation of these planets. Below the Roche limit (within a certain vicinity to the planet), these particles could not join together to form satellites and would consequently settle into orbital rings.

Satellites

Each of the giant planets possesses a number of satellites. Jupiter has sixteen known satellites—they are grouped according to size. Each of the four largest satellites of Jupiter exhibits evidence of internal activity at some point in their evolutions. In fact, Io, the densest satellite and the one closest to Jupiter, is the only celestial body besides Earth known to be currently volcanically active. Saturn has 21 satellites. Titan, the second-largest known satellite, has its own atmosphere. The other six largest of Saturn's satellites all have icy surfaces; some of these show evidence of past internal activity. The smaller 14 are relatively unknown. Uranus has five satellites. Each of them displays evidence of geological activity, in the form of valleys, smoothed surfaces, cliffs, mountains, and depressions. Neptune has eight known satellites. The larger, Triton, is similar to Titan in that it has an atmosphere. The other seven satellites of Neptune are relatively unknown.

Pluto and Charon

Though Charon was originally considered a satellite of Pluto, the ninth planet in the solar system, it now appears that the two are more accurately described as a double-planet system (largely because of the similarity in the sizes of the two). It is believed that these bodies formed from the solar nebula like most other objects in the solar system. Pluto has a highly irregular orbit, which places it closer to the Sun than Neptune for periods of time. In sharp contrast to its giant neighbors, this planet's density is higher than that of water ice. The surface of Pluto consists of high levels of methane absorbed into ice, with trace amounts of carbon oxide and nitrogen. Charon resembles the major uranian satellites more so than it does Pluto. It consists of water ice with a siliceous or hydrocarbonate contaminant.

Kepler's laws

Kepler's laws are a collection of observations about the motion of planets in the solar system. Formulated by Johannes Kepler in the 1600s, these laws are still vital to our understanding of the way the universe works. Kepler's first law states that each planet moves in its own elliptical path and that all of these orbits have the Sun as their singular focal point. Before Kepler's discovery, astronomers had assumed that planetary orbits were circular (because the heavens were assumed to be geometrically perfect). Kepler's second law says that a straight line between a planet and the Sun sweeps out equal areas in equal time. In other words, planets move quickest in the part of their orbit that is closest to the Sun, and vice versa. Kepler's third law states that the further a planet is from the Sun, the longer its orbital period will be. In mathematical terms, the square of a planet's period is inversely proportional to the cube of the radius of its orbit.

Stellar observation

The observation of stars relates to one of three stellar properties: position, brightness, and spectra. Positional stellar observation is principally performed through study of the positions of stars on multiple photographic plates. Historically, this type of analysis was done through measurement of the angular positions of the stars in the sky. Parallax of a star is its apparent shift in position due to the revolution of the Earth about the Sun; this property can be used to establish the distance to a star. Observation of the brightness of a star involves the categorization of stars according to their magnitudes. There is a fixed intensity ratio between each of the six magnitudes. Since stars emit light over a range of wavelengths, viewing a star at different wavelengths can give an indication of its temperature. The analysis of stars' spectra provides information about the temperatures of stars—the higher a star's temperature, the more ionized the gas in its outer layer. A star's spectrum also relates to its chemical composition.

Binary star

Binary star systems, of which about fifty percent of the stars in the sky are members, consist of two stars that orbit each other. The orbits of and distances between members of a binary system vary. A visual binary is a pair of stars that can be visually observed. Positional measurements of a visual binary reveal the orbital paths of the two stars. Astronomers can identify astrometric binaries through long-term observation of a visible star—if the star appears to wobble, it may be inferred that it is orbiting a companion star that is not visible. An eclipsing binary can be identified through observation of the brightness of a star. Variations in the visual brightness of a star can occur when one star in a binary system passes in front of the other. Sometimes, variations in the spectral lines of a star occur because it is in a binary system. This type of binary is a spectroscopic binary.

(handwritten margin note: luminosity; high temp; white dwarfs; Giants; spectral class)

Hertzsprung-Russell diagram

The Hertzsprung-Russell (H-R) diagram was developed to explore the relationships between the luminosities and spectral qualities of stars. This diagram involves plotting these qualities on a graph, with absolute magnitude (luminosity) on the vertical and spectral class on the horizontal. Plotting a number of stars on the H-R diagram demonstrates that stars fall into narrowly defined regions, which correspond to stages in stellar evolution. Most stars are situated in a diagonal strip that runs from the top-left (high temperature, high luminosity) to the lower-right (low temperature, low luminosity). This diagonal line shows stars in the main sequence of evolution (often called dwarfs). Stars that fall above this line on the diagram (low temperature, high luminosity) are believed to be much larger than the stars on the main sequence (because their high luminosities are not due to higher temperatures than main sequence stars); they are termed giants and supergiants. Stars below the main sequence (high temperature, low luminosity) are called white dwarfs. The H-R diagram is useful in calculating distances to stars.

Stellar evolution

The life cycle of a star is closely related to its mass—low-mass stars become white dwarfs, while high-mass stars become supernovae. A star is born when a protostar is formed from a collapsing interstellar cloud. The temperature at the center of the protostar rises, allowing nucleosynthesis to begin. Nucleosynthesis, or hydrogen-burning through fusion, entails a release of energy. Eventually, the star runs out of fuel (hydrogen). If the star is relatively low mass, the disruption of hydrostatic equilibrium allows the star to contract due to gravity. This raises the temperature just outside the core to a point at which nucleosynthesis and a different kind of fusion (with helium as fuel) that produces a carbon nucleus can occur. The star swells with greater energy, becoming a red giant. Once this phase is over, gravity becomes active again, shrinking the star until the degeneracy pressure of electrons begins to operate, creating a white dwarf that will eventually burn out. If the star has a high mass, the depletion of hydrogen creates a supernova.

Supernova

When a star on the main sequence runs out of hydrogen fuel, it begins to burn helium (the by-product of nucleosynthesis). Once helium-burning is complete in a massive star, the mass causes the core temperature to rise, enabling the fusion of carbon, then silicon, and a succession of other atomic nuclei, each of which takes place in a new shell further out of the core. When the fusion cycle reaches iron (which cannot serve as fuel for a nuclear reaction), an iron core begins to form, which accumulates over time. Eventually, the temperature and pressure in the core become high enough for electrons to interact with protons in the iron nuclei to produce neutrons. In a matter of moments, this reaction is complete. The core falls and collides with the star's outer envelope, causing a massive explosion (a supernova). This continues until the neutrons exert degeneracy pressure; this

(handwritten margin notes: red giant; white dwarf; supernova; He ↓ fusion ↓ on ↓ neutrons ↓ core falls ↓ supernova → pulsar → massive stars → Black Hole)

creates a pulsar. In more massive stars, nothing can stop the collapse, which ends in the creation of a black hole.

Meteoroid

A meteoroid is a small, solid fragment of material in the solar system. An enormous number of these objects are present in the system. The term meteor is used to refer to such a body when it enters the Earth's atmosphere. Interaction (friction) between meteors and the upper levels of the atmosphere cause them to break up; most disintegrate before they reach the surface. The heat associated with frictional forces causes meteors to glow, creating the phenomena of shooting stars. The meteors that are large enough to avoid complete disintegration, and can therefore travel all the way down through the atmosphere to Earth's surface, are termed meteorites. Analysis of these fragments indicates that these bodies originate from the Moon, Mars, comets, and small asteroids that cross Earth's orbital path. The forceful impacts of meteorites on Earth's surface compress, heat, and vaporize some of the materials of the meteorite as well as crustal materials, producing gases and water vapor.

Asteroid

An asteroid is a small, solid planet (planetoid) that orbits the Sun. The orbital paths of most asteroids are between the orbits of Jupiter and Mars. Many of these bodies have been studied extensively and given names; those in the main belt (which tend to be carbonaceous) are classified into subgroups based on their distance from a large, named asteroid (for example, Floras, Hildas, Cybeles). Atens are asteroids whose orbits lie between the Earth and the Sun, and Apollos are asteroids with orbits that mimic Earth's. Asteroids may also be classified based on their composition. C-type asteroids exhibit compositions similar to that of the Sun and are fairly dark. S-type asteroids are made up of nickel-iron and iron- and magnesium-silicates; these are relatively bright. Bright asteroids made up exclusively of nickel iron are classified as M-type. Observation of the relative brightness of an asteroid allows astronomers to estimate its size.

Interstellar medium

The interstellar, or interplanetary, medium (the space between planets and stars) is populated by comets, asteroids, and meteoroids. However, particles exist in this medium on an even smaller scale. Tiny solid bodies (close to a millionth of a meter in diameter) are called interplanetary dust. The accumulation of this material in arctic lakes, for example, allows scientists to study it. Such analysis has revealed that these grains are most likely miniscule fragments of the nuclei of dead comets. They possess low density, for they are really many microscopic particles stuck together. The interplanetary dust refracts sunlight, which produces a visible (but faint) glow in parts of the sky populated by clouds of this dust. The interstellar medium also contains particle remnants of dead stars and gases (such as hydrogen molecules ionized by ultraviolet photons). Black holes (objects that collapse under their own gravitational forces), which trap photons, are also believed to populate the interstellar medium. Black holes are a form of dark matter.

Dark matter

Observations of the gravitational force in the solar system (based on Kepler's laws) have indicated for years that there are bodies in the system that we cannot see. Dark matter (sometimes called missing matter) is thought to account for the unseen masses, though its exact nature is unknown. Some dark matter may simply be ordinary celestial bodies too small to be observed from Earth, even with technology such as high-powered telescopes. The presence of MACHOs (massive compact halo objects) has been noted through observation of distant galaxies—at certain times astronomers can discern dips in the brightness of these galaxies, thought to be caused by a large object (a MACHO) passing between Earth and the galaxy under observation. Some have postulated that dark matter is made up of WIMPs (weakly interacting massive particles), which do not interact with photons or other forms of electromagnetic radiation; these particles are hypothetical, because astronomers cannot detect or study them.

Eclipses

Eclipses occur when one celestial body obscures the view of another, either partially or completely. A solar eclipse, or eclipse of the Sun by the Moon, happens when the Moon passes directly in front of the Sun (as observed from Earth). Alternately, a lunar eclipse occurs when the Moon is situated in the Earth's shadow and is therefore completely invisible. These events do not happen every month because of the differential between the orbital planes of the Moon and the Earth—the Moon's orbit is about five degrees off from the ecliptic. The Moon's orbital path is subject to the same precession that occurs in the Earth's rotational axis; this causes the occasional intersection of the orbital planes of the two bodies. Therefore, eclipses are produced by a combination of the effects of the precession of the Moon's orbit, the orbit itself, and the Earth's orbit.

Newton's law of gravitation

Newton's law of gravitation (sometimes referred to as the law of universal gravitation) states that the force of gravity operates as an attractive force between all bodies in the universe. Prior to Newton's formulation of this law, scientists believed that two gravitational forces were at work in the universe—that gravity operated differently on Earth than it did in space. Newton's discovery served to unify these two conceptions of gravity. This law is expressed as a mathematical formula: $F = GMm/D2$, in which F is the gravitational force, M and m are the masses of two bodies, D is the distance between them, and G is the gravitational constant (6.67×10^{-11}). The gravitational attraction between two objects, therefore, depends on the distance between them and their relative masses. Newton's law of gravitation served to clarify the mechanisms by which Kepler's laws operated. In effect, Newton proved Kepler's laws to be true through the development of this law.

Milky Way

The Milky Way, which houses the Earth's solar system, is a spiral galaxy. It consists of a central bulging disk, the center of which is referred to as a nucleus. Most of a galaxy's visible light comes from stars in this region. The disk is surrounded by a halo of stars and star clusters that spread above, next to, and beneath the nucleus. Globular clusters (dense, spherical clusters of ancient stars) are often found in the halo. Spiral arms of high-luminosity stars (from which this type of galaxy gets its name) fan out from the nucleus as well, with stars that are less bright in between. Interstellar dust populates the entire galaxy between celestial bodies. The entire galaxy rotates about the center. While Earth, the Sun, and its solar system are located on the disk, we are far from the center of the Milky Way. The galaxy's mass, determined through the application of Kepler's third law to the Sun's orbit, is about 1,011 solar masses.

Structures of galaxies

Elliptical galaxies are roughly spherical. Within this category, subgroups based on the degree of flattening exhibited in the galaxy's shape range from E0 (spherical) to E7 (flat). A dwarf elliptical galaxy has a spheroidal shape, with low mass and low luminosity. An S0 galaxy is similar in shape to a spiral galaxy, but lacks spiral arms. Spiral galaxies such as the Milky Way are characterized by disk-like nuclei with spiral arms. Subtypes of this category are determined by the tightness of the spiral arms and the size of the nucleus; a spiral galaxy of Sa type has a large nucleus and tightly wound arms, and an Sc-type galaxy consists of a small nucleus with open spiral arms. A barred spiral galaxy exhibits an elongated nucleus. The subtypes of barred spiral galaxies are determined like those of spiral galaxies. Some irregular galaxies (type I) display a loose spiral structure with high levels of disorganization. Other irregular galaxies (type II) can be of any shape.

Model of the inflationary universe

Hubble's law states that the speed at which a galaxy appears to be moving away from the Earth is proportional to its distance from Earth. This relatively simple formula ($v = Hr$, where v is the velocity of a receding galaxy, r is its distance from Earth, and H is the Hubble constant) had an important implication at the time that it was developed—the universe is expanding. This fact, in turn, implies that the universe began at a specific point in the past. This model suggests that a random conglomeration of quarks and leptons, along with the strong force (all the forces in the universe unified as one), existed in the very dense, very hot, early universe. When the universe was a certain age (about 10–35 seconds old), the strong force separated out from the mass. This enabled the rapid expansion of the particles that formed the universe.

Big bang theory

The theory of the big bang expands upon the model of the inflationary universe. This theory hypothesizes that the early universe consisted of elementary particles, high energy density and high levels of pressure and heat. This single mass experienced a phase change (similar to that of freezing water) when it cooled and expanded. This transition caused the early universe to expand exponentially; this period of growth is called cosmic inflation. As it continued to grow, the temperature continued to fall. At some point, baryogenesis (an unknown process in which quarks and gluons become baryons, such as protons and neutrons) occurred, somehow creating the distinction between matter and antimatter. As the universe continued to cool, the elementary forces reached their present form, and elementary particles engaged in big bang nucleosynthesis (a process that produced helium and deuterium nuclei). Gravity became the predominant force governing interactions between particles; this enabled increasing accretion of particles of matter, which eventually formed the universal constituents as we recognize them today.

Practice Test

Multiple Choice Questions

1. Which of the following statements correctly describes a similarity or difference between rocks and minerals?
    a. Minerals may contain traces of organic compounds, while rocks do not.
    b. Rocks are classified by their formation and the minerals they contain, while minerals are classified by their chemical composition and physical properties.
    c. Both rocks and minerals can be polymorphs.
    d. Both rocks and minerals may contain mineraloids.

2. Which of the following is the best description of mineraloids?
    a. Mineraloids are organic compounds found in rocks.
    b. Mineraloids are inorganic solids containing two or more minerals with different crystalline structures.
    c. Mineraloids are inorganic solids containing one or more minerals with the same crystalline structure.
    d. Mineraloids are minerals that lack a crystalline structure.

3. All of the following are branches of petrology EXCEPT:
    a. Metamorphic petrology.
    b. Igneous petrology.
    c. Mineralogical petrology.
    d. Sedimentary petrology.

4. Which of the following is NOT one of the five major physical properties of minerals?
    a. Chemical composition
    b. Hardness
    c. Luster
    d. Streak

5. Which of these minerals would have the lowest score on the Mohs scale?
    a. Gypsum
    b. Fluorite
    c. Talc
    d. Diamond

6. A mineral's true color is observed by:
    a. Conducting a streak test on white paper.
    b. Conducting a streak test on unglazed porcelain tile.
    c. Inspecting the mineral's outer surface.
    d. Shining a light on the mineral to inspect its luster.

- 98 -

7. Galena, pyrite, and magnetite are examples of minerals with which of the following types of luster?
    a. Pearly
    b. Greasy
    c. Adamantine
    d. Metallic

8. According to the Dana classification system, gold, silver, and copper belong to which class?
    a. Organic
    b. Elemental
    c. Oxide
    d. Sulfide

9. According to the Dana classification system, minerals that contain the anion SO_4^{2-} are part of which chemical class?
    a. Sulfate
    b. Sulfite
    c. Halide
    d. Phosphate

10. Minerals that form on the sea floor from discarded shells are most likely part of which chemical class?
    a. Sulfate
    b. Organic
    c. Carbonate
    d. Silicate

11. The lithification process results in the formation of which of the following types of rocks?
    a. Sedimentary
    b. Intrusive igneous
    c. Extrusive igneous
    d. Metamorphic

12. Which of the following types of igneous rock solidifies deepest beneath the Earth's surface?
    a. Hypabyssal
    b. Plutonic
    c. Volcanic
    d. Detrital

13. Which of the following factors directly contributes to soil erosion?
    a. Air pollution from cars and factories
    b. Use of pesticides
    c. Deforestation and overgrazing
    d. Water pollution caused by excess sedimentation

14. Physical weathering of rocks can be caused by all of the following EXCEPT:
    a. The freezing and thawing of water on the surface of rocks.
    b. Changes in temperature.
    c. Oxidation.
    d. Changes in pressure due to the removal of overlying rocks.

15. Which of the following is NOT an example of chemical weathering of rocks?
    a. Highly acidic rainwater causes dissolution of rocks.
    b. Minerals that comprise rocks take on water, causing them to enlarge and creating fractures within the rocks.
    c. Salt water penetrates fractures in rocks and leaves behind salt crystals that cause fractures.
    d. Iron molecules in rocks react with atmospheric oxygen, which causes oxidation.

16. Which of the following lists places several phases of the sedimentary cycle in the correct order?
    a. Erosion, weathering, transportation, deposition
    b. Weathering, erosion, deposition, transportation
    c. Weathering, deposition, erosion, transportation
    d. Weathering, erosion, transportation, deposition

17. Which of the following is required for the process of diagenesis (also called lithification)?
    a. Magma
    b. Water
    c. Wind
    d. Sulfur

18. Nondetrital sedimentary rock is produced by:
    a. Chemical precipitation.
    b. Cooling of magma just below the Earth's surface.
    c. Physical weathering processes.
    d. Weathering of igneous rock.

19. Leaching in the "A" soil horizon results from:
    a. The accumulation of cations in the "B" horizon.
    b. The accumulation of cations in the "O" horizon.
    c. Contact with acid solutions generated in the "O" horizon.
    d. Contact with acid solutions generated in the "B" horizon.

20. Which of the following statements is true of rocks such as olivine that are found at the top of Bowen's reaction series?
    a. They are classified as metamorphic.
    b. They weather more quickly than rocks found lower in the series.
    c. They crystallize at lower temperatures than rocks found at the bottom of the series.
    d. None of the above

21. Metamorphic rock is produced when which of the following undergoes profound changes as a result of exposure to intense pressure and heat?
    a. A batholith
    b. A protolith
    c. A subduction zone
    d. A volcano

22. All of the following are examples of metamorphic rocks EXCEPT:
    a. Granite.
    b. Quartzite.
    c. Slate.
    d. Marble.

23. When metamorphic rock is stressed unevenly during recrystallization, it can result in:
    a. Foliation.
    b. Contact metamorphism.
    c. Regional metamorphism.
    d. Extrusion.

24. Which of the following statements correctly describes a distinction between regional and contact metamorphism?
    a. Regional metamorphism results from intense heat, while contact metamorphism is caused by extreme pressure.
    b. Regional metamorphism results from extreme pressure, while contact metamorphism is caused by intense heat.
    c. Regional metamorphism occurs when magma is injected into surrounding rock, while contact metamorphism occurs when a large area of rock is subjected to intense heat and pressure.
    d. Regional metamorphism occurs when a large area of rock is subjected to intense heat and pressure, while contact metamorphism occurs when magma is injected into surrounding rock.

25. When two tectonic plates are moving laterally in opposing directions, this is called a:
    a. Transformational boundary.
    b. Compressional boundary.
    c. Oppositional boundary.
    d. Lateral boundary.

26. Which of the following statements correctly describes a difference between the lithosphere and the asthenosphere?
    a. The asthenosphere is comprised of atmospheric gas, while the lithosphere is composed of liquids and solids.
    b. The asthenosphere is hotter and more fluid than the lithosphere.
    c. The lithosphere is hotter and has a different chemical composition than the asthenosphere.
    d. Heat is transferred through conduction in the asthenosphere, while it is transferred through convection in the lithosphere.

27. The most recently formed parts of the Earth's crust can be found at:
    a. Subduction zones.
    b. Compressional boundaries.
    c. Extensional boundaries.
    d. Mid-ocean ridges.

28. When an earthquake occurs, the "shaking" that is observed results directly from:
    a. Static deformation.
    b. Seismic waves.
    c. Compression waves.
    d. Continental drift.

29. Which of the following events immediately precedes a volcanic eruption?
    a. A batholith forms beneath the Earth's surface.
    b. Magma fills vertical and horizontal fractures in the Earth's crust, creating sills and dykes.
    c. An oceanic plate is subducted by a continental plate.
    d. A dyke reaches the Earth's surface and a plume passes through it.

30. Cinder cone volcanoes are created by:
    a. A series of explosive eruptions.
    b. Gradual eruptions over time.
    c. A combination of both explosive and gradual eruptions over time.
    d. None of the above

31. Island chains like the Hawaiian or Midway Islands are created when:
    a. Tectonic plates move apart and magma rises to the surface.
    b. The subduction process creates magma, which rises above the ocean's surface to form islands.
    c. Underwater earthquakes produce mountains that protrude above the water's surface.
    d. A tectonic plate gradually moves over a fixed plume of magma that rises from the mantle.

32. Which of the following is true of a volcano that is thought to be dormant?
    a. It will probably never erupt again, and it is quite safe for people to live near its base.
    b. It is expected to erupt some time again in the future, but danger is not imminent.
    c. It is expected to erupt soon, and evacuation should be commenced.
    d. It is a shield volcano that is erupting, but people living near the volcano should not expect their lives to be significantly disrupted.

33. The mountain in Figure 1 has the oldest rock in its core and the youngest rock in its outer layers. Which of the following terms best describes the mountain?
    a. Syncline
    b. Anticline
    c. Fault-block
    d. Graben

Figure 1.

34. When fault-block mountains like those in the Western United States are formed, sections that are lifted by tensional forces are called:
    a. Antiforms.
    b. Faces.
    c. Horsts.
    d. Rifts.

35. Which of the following is thought to be a direct result of the Dynamo Effect?
    a. The motion of tectonic plates over the mantle
    b. The heating of the Earth's atmosphere
    c. The production of the Earth's magnetic field
    d. None of the above

36. The Earth's magnetic field protects it from:
    a. Excess heat from the Sun.
    b. Radio waves from black holes.
    c. Solar wind.
    d. Impacts from space debris.

37. In 1912, Alfred Wegener proposed that:
    a. The Earth's magnetic poles have reversed several times throughout history.
    b. Tectonic plates move because of convection currents in the mantle.
    c. Mountains are formed by tectonic plates pushing against one another.
    d. The continents once formed a single land mass, but have since drifted apart.

38. The Richter scale determines the magnitude of an earthquake by:
    a. Comparing its destructiveness to that of other earthquakes.
    b. Measuring the amount of seismic energy it releases.
    c. Ascertaining the farthest distance from the epicenter at which the earthquake can be felt.
    d. Measuring the depth of the earthquake.

39. An earthquake with a Richter magnitude of 1.5 can be expected to have which of the following effects on an urban area with high standards for building construction?
    a. The earthquake will probably not be felt, and will not cause damage.
    b. There may be slight damage to well-constructed buildings over a small area.
    c. There will be serious damage to well-constructed buildings over a large area.
    d. There will be catastrophic damage and many people will be injured.

40. The process that causes lithospheric plates to move over the surface of the mantle is called:
    a. Conduction.
    b. Convection.
    c. Tension.
    d. Subduction.

41. Which of the following statements correctly describes the relationship between temperature and density in water?

    a. As the temperature of liquid water decreases, density decreases monotonically.

    b. As the temperature of frozen water (ice) increases, density decreases monotonically.

    c. Water in the solid state generally has a higher density than water in the liquid state.

    d. Water in the liquid state generally has a higher density than water in the solid state.

42. Water's specific heat capacity is second only to that of ammonia. This means that:

    a. Water vaporizes at a higher temperature than ammonia.

    b. It takes more energy to increase the temperature of ammonia than it does to increase the temperature of water.

    c. Water is always denser than ammonia.

    d. Water is only denser than ammonia at higher temperatures.

43. Water that evaporates from oceans can precipitate over land due to the process of:

    a. Transpiration.

    b. Advection.

    c. Sublimation.

    d. Interception.

44. Water is likely to have the shortest residence time in which of the following types of reservoirs?

    a. A glacier

    b. A lake

    c. A river

    d. The atmosphere

45. When water changes directly from a solid to a gas, skipping the liquid state, this is called:

    a. Evapotranspiration.

    b. Condensation.

    c. Sublimation.

    d. Runoff.

46. The main manmade cause of "dead zones" in portions of oceans and lakes that normally host abundant aquatic life is:

    a. Evaporation.

    b. Invasive species.

    c. Use of chemical fertilizers.

    d. Global warming.

47. The majority of the solar energy that reaches Earth is absorbed by:
    a. Glaciers.
    b. Landmasses.
    c. Oceans.
    d. The Earth's atmosphere.

48. The majority of weather phenomena occur in which part of the Earth's atmosphere?
    a. Troposphere
    b. Stratosphere
    c. Hydrosphere
    d. Ionosphere

49. According to the Köppen Climate Classification System, regions with continental climates are most commonly found:
    a. In the interior regions of large landmasses.
    b. Near the equator.
    c. Near the Earth's poles.
    d. In places with high temperatures year-round.

50. Tropical climate zones are characterized by:
    a. Extreme temperature variations between night and day.
    b. Extreme temperature variations between seasons.
    c. Frequent rainfall.
    d. All of the above

51. Which of the following is a true statement about the Earth's oceans?
    a. Oceans comprise about 50 percent of the Earth's surface.
    b. The deepest point in the ocean is about 6,000 meters below sea level.
    c. The ocean is divided geographically into four areas: the Atlantic, Pacific, Mediterranean, and Indian.
    d. The ocean's salinity is usually between 34 and 35 parts per thousand, or 200 parts per million.

52. A guyot is defined as:
    a. Any undersea mountain more than 1,000 meters high.
    b. A seamount with a flattened top.
    c. An undersea mountain chain.
    d. A trough in the ocean floor.

53. Approximately 96.5 percent of seawater is comprised of:
    a. Hydrogen and sodium.
    b. Hydrogen and oxygen.
    c. Oxygen and sodium.
    d. Chlorine and sodium.

54. Which of the following statements correctly describes a difference between surface and subsurface ocean currents?

    a. Subsurface currents are caused only by temperature variations, while surface currents are caused by changes in air pressure.

    b. Subsurface currents are caused by temperature and density variations, while surface currents are caused by changes in air pressure.

    c. Subsurface currents are caused by temperature and density variations, while surface currents are caused by wind.

    d. Surface currents are caused by changes in air temperature, while subsurface currents are caused by changes in water temperature.

55. The Coriolis effect in the Earth's oceans is caused by:

    a. The Earth's rotation.

    b. The Earth's magnetic field.

    c. Variations in the density of seawater.

    d. The Gulf Stream.

56. Which of the following statements correctly describes an effect of the Gulf Stream?

    a. It increases humidity along North America's west coast.

    b. It makes the climate of South America colder.

    c. It makes the climate of Northern Europe warmer.

    d. It makes the climate of the Caribbean milder and less humid.

57. Thermohaline circulation is caused by:

    a. Temperature differences between seawater only.

    b. Salinity differences between seawater only.

    c. Variations in seawater density caused by both temperature and salinity differences.

    d. None of the above

58. When cold, nutrient-rich water is allowed to rise to the surface because winds parallel to a landmass's coast blow the surface water towards the open sea, this is called:

    a. Ekman transport.

    b. The Coriolis effect.

    c. Upwelling.

    d. Downwelling.

59. The frequency of ocean waves is measured by:

    a. The distance between a wave's crest and trough.

    b. The distance between the crests of two subsequent waves.

    c. The time between two subsequent wave crests.

    d. The number of wave crests that pass a given point each second.

60. When the accumulation of snow and ice exceeds ablation, which of the following occurs as a direct result?
    a. An iceberg breaks free from a glacier.
    b. A glacier gradually forms.
    c. A glacier slowly erodes.
    d. A lake forms within a glacier.

61. The Cretaceous-Tertiary Event, during which non-avian dinosaurs became extinct, occurred approximately how long ago?
    a. 10,000 years ago
    b. 15.5 million years ago
    c. 38 million years ago
    d. 65.5 million years ago

62. Which of the following techniques is NOT a radiometric dating process?
    a. Potassium-argon dating
    b. Stratigraphic dating
    c. Uranium-lead dating
    d. Chlorine-36 dating

63. In the field of geology, the term "uniformitarianism" refers to the belief that:
    a. Catastrophic events like mass extinctions are the main forces that have shaped the Earth.
    b. The Earth's crust has not undergone any dramatic changes since its formation.
    c. The natural forces that shape the Earth have remained relatively constant over geologic time.
    d. The Earth's stratigraphy is more or less uniform at any given geographic location.

64. In the field of stratigraphy, the relative ages of rocks may be determined by examining which of the following types of evidence?
    a. The dates the rocks were formed and the ages of fossils deposited within the rocks
    b. Evidence of changes in detrital remanent magnetism when the rock was deposited
    c. The vertical layering pattern of the rock
    d. All of the above

65. Which of the following is an example of an absolute age?
    a. A fossil is 37 million years old.
    b. A rock is less than 100,000 years old.
    c. An organic artifact is between 5,000 and 10,000 years old.
    d. All of the above

66. In geochronology, which of the following is the longest time period?
    a. An epoch
    b. An era
    c. An eon
    d. An age

67. Which of the following correctly lists the periods that comprise the Mesozoic era, from earliest to most recent?
    a. Jurassic, Triassic, Cretaceous
    b. Permian, Triassic, Jurassic
    c. Triassic, Jurassic, Cretaceous
    d. Triassic, Jurassic, Permian

68. In his work, *The Origin of Life*, Alexander Oparin argued that:
    a. Life arose spontaneously from other decaying organic matter.
    b. Life originated in deep-sea vents.
    c. Life arose on Earth through a "primordial soup" that is no longer possible because of atmospheric oxygen.
    d. Life emerged as part of an autocatalytic network.

69. According to current theories, the Earth was formed approximately how long ago?
    a. 50 million years ago
    b. 1.25 billion years ago
    c. 4.5 billion years ago
    d. 15 billion years ago

70. The most severe mass extinction event in Earth's history was the:
    a. Cretaceous-Tertiary Event.
    b. Permian-Triassic Event.
    c. Ordovician-Silurian Event.
    d. Late Devonian Event.

71. Which of the following life forms appeared first on Earth?
    a. Eukaryotes
    b. Arthropods
    c. Prokaryotes
    d. Amphibians

72. The Cambrian Explosion is best described as:
    a. A great migration of flora and fauna between North and South America that vastly increased biodiversity on both continents.
    b. The emergence of multicellular life about one billion years ago.
    c. The increase in the pace of evolution ushered in by the emergence of sexual reproduction about 1.2 billion years ago.
    d. The dramatic increase in biodiversity that began about 530 million years ago and resulted in the emergence of complex animals over a period of millions of years.

73. Which of the following is considered observational evidence in support of the Big Bang Theory?
    a. Expansion in the redshifts of galaxies
    b. Measurements of cosmic microwave background radiation
    c. Measurements of the distribution of quasars and galaxies
    d. All of the above

74. The Cosmological Principle is best described as:
    a. An assumption that cannot be tested empirically because it has no observable implications.
    b. A scientific hypothesis that has been repeatedly validated in empirical tests.
    c. A working assumption that has testable structural consequences.
    d. A law of physics that defies empirical testing.

75. Redshift is observed when:
    a. A light-emitting object moves away from an observer.
    b. A star begins to decrease the amount of light it emits.
    c. A light-emitting object moves toward an observer.
    d. A magnetic field bends observed light.

76. Which of the following statements best describes the physical structure of the universe?
    a. Galaxies are the largest structures in the universe, and they are distributed evenly throughout space.
    b. Superclusters are the largest structures in the universe, and they are distributed evenly throughout space.
    c. Superclusters are the largest structures in the universe, and they are unevenly distributed so that large voids exist in space.
    d. Filaments are the largest structures in the universe, and they surround large, bubble-like voids.

77. Which of the following statements about galaxies is true?
    a. Galaxies are the only structures in the universe that do not contain dark matter.
    b. Galaxies are gravitationally bound, meaning structures within the galaxy orbit around its center.
    c. Galaxies typically contain over one trillion stars.
    d. Galaxies are comprised of clusters and superclusters.

78. The structure of the Milky Way galaxy is best described as:
    a. Spiral.
    b. Starburst.
    c. Elliptical.
    d. Irregular.

79. The Hertzsprung-Russell (H-R) Diagram is used primarily to:
    a. Determine a star's age by comparing its temperature and luminosity.
    b. Measure a star's size by estimating its luminosity.
    c. Determine a galaxy's luminosity when its size is known.
    d. Group galaxies by their morphological types.

80. The distance from the Earth to the Sun is equal to one:
    a. Astronomical unit.
    b. Light year.
    c. Parsec.
    d. Arcsecond.

81. The energy radiated by stars is produced by:
    a. Neutronicity.
    b. Nuclear fusion.
    c. Nuclear fission.
    d. Gravitational confinement.

82. The stream of charged particles that escape the Sun's gravitational pull is best described by which of the following terms?
    a. Solar wind
    b. Solar flare
    c. Solar radiation
    d. Sunspots

83. Which of the following planets in our solar system is NOT a gas giant?
    a. Saturn
    b. Neptune
    c. Venus
    d. Jupiter

84. The asteroid belt in our solar system is located between:
    a. Earth and Mars.
    b. Neptune and Pluto.
    c. Uranus and Saturn.
    d. Mars and Jupiter.

85. Which of the following is a proposed explanation for the formation of black holes?
    a. High-energy collisions
    b. Gravitational collapse
    c. Accretion of matter
    d. A and B

86. A total solar eclipse can be observed only by viewers located:
    a. Within the penumbra but outside of the umbra.
    b. Within the umbra.
    c. Within either the umbra or the penumbra.
    d. Outside of the Moon's penumbra.

87. The atomic number of an element is defined by:
    a. The total number of protons and electrons it contains.
    b. The total number of electrons it contains.
    c. The total number of protons it contains.
    d. The total number of neutrons it contains.

88. Which of the following statements best describes the main distinction between the isotopes carbon-12 and carbon-13?
    a. They have different atomic numbers.
    b. They have different mass numbers.
    c. They have experienced different degrees of radioactive decay.
    d. A and B

89. Which of the following statements is NOT true of electrons?
    a. They comprise only a tiny fraction of an atom's mass.
    b. They are arranged in levels, and usually occupy the lowest energy level possible.
    c. They are negatively charged.
    d. They have a substructure that includes a nucleus.

90. Chemical compounds are formed when:
    a. Valence electrons from atoms of two different elements are shared or transferred.
    b. Valence electrons from multiple atoms of a single element are shared or transferred.
    c. The nuclei of two atoms are joined together.
    d. The nucleus of an atom is split.

- 112 -

91. The state of matter in which atoms have the strongest bond is:
    a. Plasma.
    b. Liquid.
    c. Solid.
    d. Gas.

92. Which of the following statements is true of a closed thermodynamic system?
    a. It cannot exchange heat, work, or matter with its surrounding environment.
    b. It can exchange heat and work, but not matter, with its surrounding environment.
    c. It can exchange heat, but not work or matter, with its surrounding environment.
    d. It can exchange matter, but not heat or work, with its surrounding environment.

93. The formula for calculating kinetic energy is:
    a. ½ mv2.
    b. ½ mv.
    c. mgh.
    d. mgv.

94. Which law of classical thermodynamics states that energy can neither be created nor destroyed?
    a. Zeroth
    b. First
    c. Second
    d. Third

95. James Hutton is best known for:
    a. Establishing the first observable evidence for the Big Bang Theory.
    b. Suggesting the Third Law of Thermodynamics.
    c. Proposing the theory of uniformitarianism.
    d. Introducing the Law of Superposition.

96. Which of the following is the correct formula for converting Fahrenheit to Celsius?
    a. 5/9 (F - 32)
    b. 9/5 (F - 32)
    c. 5/9 (F + 32)
    d. None of the above

97. A calorimeter is used to measure changes in:
    a. Heat.
    b. Mass.
    c. Weight.
    d. Volume.

98. Commercial nuclear reactors generate electricity through the process of:
    a. Nuclear fission.
    b. Nuclear fusion.
    c. Nuclear depletion.
    d. Radioactive decay.

99. Which of the following can be inferred based on the results of the regression analysis shown in Figure 2?
    a. A change in the independent variable causes a change in the dependent variable.
    b. A change in the dependent variable causes a change in the independent variable.
    c. There is a weak positive correlation between the two variables.
    d. There is a weak negative correlation between the two variables.

Figure 2.

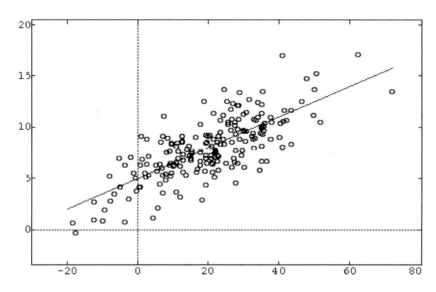

100. Random error could be caused by which of the following problems?
    a. Imperfectly calibrated equipment
    b. Extraneous disturbances that cannot be controlled
    c. Consistent human error in the use of lab equipment
    d. Failure to account for a specific variable

Answers and Explanations

1. B: It is true that rocks are classified by their formation and the minerals they contain, while minerals are classified by their chemical composition and physical properties. Answer A is incorrect because rocks may contain traces of organic compounds. Answers C and D are incorrect because only minerals can be polymorphs and only rocks contain mineraloids.

2. D: Mineraloids are best defined as minerals that lack a crystalline structure, and they are typically found in rocks. Inorganic solids containing two or more minerals with different crystalline structures are known as polymorphs.

3. C: Mineralogical petrology is not a branch of petrology. Petrologists study the various categories of rocks, including metamorphic, igneous, and sedimentary. Some petrologists, called experimental petrologists, also study changes in the geochemistry of materials that are exposed to extreme temperatures and pressures. Minerals are studied by mineralogists, not petrologists.

4. A: Chemical composition is not one of the physical properties used to classify minerals. The five major physical properties used to classify minerals are luster, hardness, cleavage, streak, and form. There is a separate classification system based on the chemical composition of minerals.

5. C: On Mohs scale of mineral hardness, talc has the lowest possible score (a one). Diamond is a ten, which is the highest possible score, and gypsum and fluorite have a score of two and four, respectively. Minerals can always scratch minerals that have a Mohs score lower than their own.

6. B: A mineral's true color is observed by conducting a streak test on unglazed porcelain tile. Paper is not appropriate for a streak test because it does not have the correct physical properties. External observation (inspecting the mineral's outer surface) is not sufficient to establish true color since streak tests sometimes reveal a color that is different from the substance's external hue. Finally, the luster test is not used to determine color.

7. D: Galena, pyrite, and magnetite are examples of minerals with a metallic luster. Opal is an example of a mineral with a greasy luster, and diamonds have an adamantine luster. Muscovite and stilbite are examples of minerals with a pearly luster. Other types of luster include dull, silky, waxy, and sub-metallic.

8. B: According to the Dana classification system, gold, silver, and copper belong to the elemental class. Members of the oxide class include chromite and magnetite, and hydrocarbons and acetates are members of the organic class. Sulfide minerals include pyrite and galena.

9. A: According to the Dana system, minerals that contain the anion SO_4^{2-} are part of the sulfate class. Sulfate minerals are typically formed in environments where highly saline water evaporates. Gypsum is an example of a mineral that belongs to the sulfate class.

10. C: Minerals that form on the sea floor from discarded shells are most likely part of the carbonate class. Minerals that form in karst regions and evaporitic settings may also be carbonates. Examples of minerals in the carbonate class include aragonite, dolomite, calcite, and siderite.

11. A: The lithification process results in the formation of sedimentary rocks. During lithification, existing rock is compacted and liquid is squeezed from its pores. Eventually, the rock is cemented together, resulting in sedimentary rock.

12. B: Plutonic, or intrusive, rock forms deep beneath the Earth's surface and cools slowly. Volcanic, or extrusive, rock solidifies at or near the surface. Hypabyssal rock forms below the Earth's surface, but not at a depth as great as plutonic rock. Detrital rock is a type of sedimentary rock.

13. C: Overgrazing and deforestation directly contribute to soil erosion by destroying the natural groundcover that normally prevents soil from being washed and blown away. These activities can ultimately result in desertification, which renders land unsuitable for agriculture.

14. C: Physical weathering of rocks can be caused by changes in temperature and pressure, as well as the freezing and thawing of water on the surfaces of rocks. Oxidation is a chemical process, not a physical one. Therefore, it is considered an example of chemical rather than physical weathering.

15. C: When salt water penetrates fractures in rocks and leaves behind salt crystals that cause the rock to fracture, it is considered physical rather than chemical weathering. Chemical weathering involves changes in the molecules that comprise the rocks, while physical weathering occurs when external factors act on the rock without changing its chemical composition in any way.

16. D: Weathering causes erosion, which often leads to transportation and the deposition of eroded material. After the eroded material is deposited in a new location, lithification proceeds and the sedimentary cycle begins anew.

17. B: Water is a key element in the lithification of sedimentary rock. After it is squeezed from the compressed material, it forms a chemical cement that holds the sedimentary rock in place. This cementation process is followed by recrystallization of the rock when equilibrium is reached.

18. A: Non-detrital sedimentary rock is produced by chemical precipitation. In contrast, detrital sedimentary rocks are comprised of pre-existing rocks, such as quartz, or weathered products of pre-existing rocks, such as clay.

19. C: Leaching in the "A" soil horizon results from contact with acid solutions generated in the "O" horizon, which is the uppermost organic layer of soil. Cations that are leached in the "A" soil horizon accumulate in the "B" soil horizon below.

20. B: Rocks such as olivine that are found at the top of Bowen's reaction series weather more quickly than rocks found lower in the series. This is because rocks high in the series crystallize at higher temperatures than those found lower in the series. This means they are less stable and more susceptible to weathering than rocks that crystallize at lower temperatures, such as quartz.

21. B: Metamorphic rock is produced when a protolith undergoes profound changes after being exposed to extreme heat and pressure. A protolith is any rock that is transformed through this process. The original rock may be sedimentary, igneous, or metamorphic. The extreme heat and pressure that serve as the catalyst for this transformation may be produced by the intrusion of magma or tectonic activity, among other factors.

22. A: Quartzite, marble, and slate are all examples of metamorphic rocks, while granite is one of the most common types of igneous rocks.

23. A: When metamorphic rock is stressed unevenly during recrystallization, it can result in foliation. Foliation is characterized by banded rock, and it occurs when certain types of minerals are reoriented during recrystallization due to uneven shortening or compression of the rock.

24. D: Regional metamorphism occurs when a large area of rock is subjected to intense heat and pressure, while contact metamorphism occurs when magma is injected into surrounding rock, also known as country rock. When contact metamorphism occurs, the rocks closest to the hot magma undergo the greatest changes.

25. A: When two tectonic plates are moving laterally in opposing directions, this is called a transform boundary. When there is friction at transform boundaries and pressure builds up, it can result in shallow earthquakes (usually at a depth of less than 25 meters). California's San Andreas Fault is an example of a transform boundary.

26. B: It is true that the asthenosphere is hotter and more fluid than the lithosphere. The asthenosphere, also called the upper mantle, is the hot, fluid layer of the Earth's mantle upon which the lithosphere, or crust, is situated. Heat is transferred within the asthenosphere through a process called convection, which sometimes causes movement in the tectonic plates that make up the lithosphere.

27. D: The most recently formed parts of the Earth's crust can be found at mid-ocean ridges. New crust forms here when magma erupts from these ridges and pushes pre-existing crust horizontally towards the continental plates. Such ridges include the Mid-Atlantic Ridge and the East Pacific Rise.

28. B: When an earthquake occurs, the "shaking" that is observed is a direct result of seismic waves. Seismic waves are powerful sound waves released when slippage between plates occurs. There are two types of seismic waves: primary, or P-waves, and secondary, or S-waves. P-waves move more quickly than S-waves, and create motion that radiates directly outward from the point of origin. S-waves produce a shearing, or side-to-side, motion.

29. D: A volcano occurs when a dyke (a vertical fracture in the Earth's crust that fills with magma) reaches the Earth's surface and a plume (a spurt of magma) passes through it. Batholiths are large masses of igneous rock that form beneath the Earth's surface, and a sill is a horizontal fracture in the Earth's crust that fills with magma. When an oceanic plate is subducted by a continental plate, it results in the formation of mountain ranges.

30. A: Cinder cone volcanoes are created by a series of explosive eruptions. Gradual eruptions produce shield volcanoes, and composite volcanoes are the result of a combination of gradual and explosive eruptions over time.

31. D: Island chains like the Hawaiian or Midway Islands are created when a tectonic plate gradually moves over a fixed plume of magma that rises from the mantle. When this plume erupts through the Earth's crust, a volcano that rises above the water's surface is formed, which creates an island. The tectonic plate gradually shifts so that the next time the fixed plume erupts, it affects a different point on the plate. This creates another volcanic island near the first one.

32. B: A volcano that is thought to be dormant is expected to erupt some time again in the future, but danger is not imminent. Dormant volcanoes are expected to erupt again in the future because they still show signs of internal volcanic activity. Extinct volcanoes are not expected to erupt again because they show no signs of activity. Active volcanoes are either erupting or about to erupt.

33. B: Since the mountain in Figure 1 has the oldest rock in its core and the youngest rock in its outer layers, it is best described as an anticline. Any mountain that results from a crustal fold and has an upward, convex shape is called an antiform. Mountains in which the rocks are progressively older from the outer layers to the core are anticlines. Synclines have downward, or concave, folds, and fault-block mountains result when faults in continental crust cause certain sections to lift or tilt. Grabens are a formation associated with fault-block mountains.

34. C: When fault-block mountains such as those in the Western United States are formed, sections that are lifted by tensional forces are called horsts. Blocks that are lowered in elevation are called grabens. The term "rift" refers to the entire area that is affected by the separation of a continental plate.

35. C: The Earth's magnetic field is thought to be produced by the Dynamo Effect. According to this theory, the Earth's rotation combined with the convection of metals within the Earth's core produce electric currents. When these currents flow through an existing magnetic field in the core, this produces a secondary magnetic field which reinforces the primary field and creates a self-sustaining dynamo.

36. C: The Earth's magnetic field protects it from solar wind. Solar wind is a stream of highly-charged radioactive particles that emanate from the Sun, and these particles are deflected by the magnetic field. The magnetic field is shaped like a bowl that covers the side of the Earth facing the Sun. It deflects most solar particles, but some are trapped in the Van Allen belt. Particularly strong bursts of solar wind allow particles to pass through this belt into the Earth's ionosphere and upper atmosphere, creating geomagnetic storms and aurora.

37. D: In 1912, Alfred Wegener proposed that the continents once formed a single land mass called Pangaea, but have since drifted apart. Theories about the Earth's magnetic fields and plate tectonics did not emerge until years later. Once they did, they helped produce evidence to support Wegener's theory.

38. B: The Richter scale determines the magnitude of an earthquake by measuring the amount of seismic energy it releases. The formula used to calculate an earthquake's Richter magnitude takes the logarithm of the horizontal amplitude of the earthquake's seismic waves into account, and also makes adjustments for the position of the seismograph relative to the earthquake.

39. A: An earthquake with a Richter magnitude of 1.5 will probably not be felt, and will not cause any damage. Earthquakes with magnitudes of less than 2.0 are usually not felt, and those with magnitudes of less than 5.0 typically do not seriously damage well-constructed buildings. Earthquakes with magnitudes of 6.0 or greater can cause damage to even well-constructed buildings.

40. B: The process that causes lithospheric plates to move over the surface of the mantle is called convection. The liquid in the lower portion of the mantle is heated by the Earth's core and rises to the surface, pushing aside cooler liquid that is already there. This liquid cools, and is in turn pushed aside by hotter liquid that has risen from below. This cycle, called convection, creates constant movement in the mantle that contributes to the motion of the tectonic plates.

41. D: Water in the liquid state generally has a higher density than water in the solid state (ice). Unlike most other substances, which become progressively denser as

they grow colder, water's density only increases until it reaches a maximum density around 4 °C, after which it begins to decrease as the temperature drops further.

42. B: The fact that water's specific heat capacity is second only to that of ammonia means that it takes more energy to increase the temperature of ammonia than it does to increase the temperature of water. Specific heat capacity refers to the amount of energy required to increase the temperature of a substance by one degree Celsius. Ammonia has the highest specific heat capacity of all substances, and the specific heat capacity of water is the second highest.

43. B: Water that evaporates from oceans can precipitate over land due to the process of advection. Water vapor is less dense than air, and this difference in density produces convection currents that move the vapor, allowing it to condense and precipitate over land masses.

44. D: Water is likely to have the shortest residence time in the atmosphere. Water molecules linger in the atmosphere for an estimated 9 days, while their residence time in glaciers may range from 20 to 100 years. Water molecules reside in lakes for approximately 50 to 100 years, and they stay in rivers for two to six months.

45. C: When water changes directly from a solid to a gas, skipping the liquid state, it is known as sublimation. It typically occurs when snow or ice is exposed to direct sunlight, and it is possible at unusually low atmospheric pressure points.

46. C: The main manmade cause of "dead zones" in portions of oceans and lakes that normally host abundant aquatic life is the use of chemical fertilizers. These fertilizers, which are high in nitrogen and phosphorous, enter lakes and rivers in water runoff and become concentrated in certain areas. This concentration, called eutrophication, eventually depletes the water's oxygen levels and renders it incapable of supporting life.

47. C: The majority of the solar energy that reaches Earth is absorbed by the oceans, which make up 71 percent of the Earth's surface. Because of water's high specific heat capacity, oceans can absorb and store large quantities of heat, thus preventing drastic increases in the overall atmospheric temperature.

48. A: The majority of weather phenomena occur in the Earth's troposphere. The troposphere is comprised of the area roughly 8-15 kilometers above the Earth's surface. It contains the majority of the mass of Earth's atmosphere and 99 percent of its water vapor.

49. A: According to the Köppen Climate Classification System, regions with continental climates are most commonly found in the interior regions of large landmasses. The continental climate is characterized by low levels of precipitation and large seasonal temperature variations.

50. C: Tropical climate zones are characterized by frequent rainfall, especially during the monsoon season, and by moderate temperatures that vary little from season to season or between night and day. Tropical zones do experience frequent rainfall, which leads to abundant vegetation.

51. D: It is true that the ocean's salinity is usually between 34 and 35 parts per thousand, or 200 parts per million. Oceans comprise about 70.8 percent of the Earth's surface, and the ocean's deepest point is over 10,000 meters below sea level. The Mediterranean is considered a sea, not an ocean.

52. B: A guyot is defined as a seamount with a flattened top. The term "seamount" refers to any undersea volcano that is more than 1,000 meters tall. Undersea troughs are called trenches, and undersea mountain chains are called mid-ocean ridges.

53. B: Approximately 96.5 percent of seawater is comprised of hydrogen and oxygen. Although seawater does contain sodium, chlorine, magnesium, sulfur, and other dissolved solids, its primary components are the same substances that make up fresh water.

54. C: It is true that subsurface currents are driven by temperature and density variations, while surface currents are driven by wind. Ocean currents affect vast quantities of seawater and strongly influence the climate of Earth's landmasses.

55. A: The appearance of the Coriolis effect in the Earth's oceans is caused by the Earth's rotation. The Coriolis effect results when free objects such as water move over a rotating surface such as the Earth. As water moves from the poles towards the Equator, it curves slightly westward, while water moving in the opposite direction (from the Equator towards the poles) moves slightly eastward.

56. C: The Gulf Stream, which is a surface current that originates in the Gulf of Mexico and travels across the Atlantic Ocean, makes the climate of Northern Europe warmer. After traveling up the eastern coast of the U.S., the Gulf Stream splits into two forks. The North Atlantic Drift travels across the ocean to warm Europe, while the southern fork travels toward West Africa.

57. C: Thermohaline circulation is caused by variations in seawater density caused by both temperature and salinity differences. This process, which affects subsurface ocean currents, contributes to the mixing of seawater and accounts for the relative uniformity of the water's physical and chemical properties.

58. C: When cold, nutrient-rich water is allowed to rise to the surface because winds parallel to a landmass's coast blow the surface water towards the open sea, it is called upwelling. Upwelling brings the remains of dead sea creatures to the surface, providing food for phytoplankton. Zooplanktons consume the phytoplankton, and

larger organisms consume the zooplanktons. Thus, upwelling allows marine life to thrive near coastal areas.

59. D: The frequency of ocean waves is measured by the number of wave crests that pass a given point each second. The crest of a wave is its highest point, and the trough is its lowest point. The distance between two subsequent crests is called wavelength, and the height is the distance between a single wave's trough and crest.

60. B: When the accumulation of snow and ice exceeds ablation, a glacier will gradually form. Ablation is the sloughing off of ice and snow through melting, evaporation, sublimation, and wind erosion. When snow and ice accumulate faster than ablation occurs, a glacier will form and continue to gain mass until the rate of ablation overtakes the rate of accumulation.

61. D: The Cretaceous-Tertiary event, during which non-avian dinosaurs became extinct, occurred approximately 65.5 million years ago during the Mesozoic era. It is the most recent of the five major extinction events that have occurred throughout the Earth's history.

62. B: Stratigraphic dating is not a radiometric dating process because it does not consider the radioactive properties of materials to estimate their dates. Instead, it relies on the Law of Superposition to estimate relative ages by comparing the relative depths of materials.

63. C: In the field of geology, the term "uniformitarianism" refers to the belief that the natural forces, laws, and processes that shape the Earth have remained relatively constant over geologic time. This belief contradicts catastrophism, which maintains that dramatic events have been the primary forces involved in shaping the Earth.

64. D: The field of stratigraphy is divided into several subfields, each of which focuses on a unique aspect of sedimentary material and yields unique insights about the material's age. In the subfield of chronostratigraphy, a material's age is estimated by determining when it was formed or deposited. The study of the vertical layering of rock types is called lithostratigraphy, and the study of fossil ages in rock layers is called biostratigraphy. Magnetostratigraphy examines data about changes in detrital remanent magnetism (DRM) at the time rocks were formed.

65. A: A fossil that is 37 million years old is an example of an absolute age. Absolute dating, which can be accomplished through the use of radiometric techniques, establishes precise ages for materials, while stratigraphic techniques only produce relative dates. Relative dating can pinpoint approximate ages for rocks and fossils based on clues in the surrounding rock, but it cannot be used to determine absolute age.

66. C: In geochronology, an eon is the longest time period, lasting at least half a billion years. An era lasts several hundred million years, an epoch measures tens of millions of years, and an age is shorter than 10 million years but longer than one million years.

67. C: The Mesozoic era is comprised of the Triassic, Jurassic, and Cretaceous periods. It was preceded by the Paleozoic era, of which the Permian is the last period. The Triassic period ended about 200 million years ago, and was followed by the Jurassic period. The Jurassic period gave way to the Cretaceous period just under 150 million years ago.

68. C: In his 1924 work, *The Origin of Life*, Alexander Oparin argued that life arose on Earth through a "primordial soup" that is no longer possible because of atmospheric oxygen.

69. C: According to current theories, the Earth was formed approximately 4.5 billion years ago. This date has been established through the use of radiometric dating performed on meteorite fossils.

70. B: The most severe mass extinction event in Earth's history was the Permian-Triassic Event. It occurred approximately 251.4 million years ago, and resulted in the extinction of 96 percent of all marine species and 70 percent of terrestrial vertebrate species.

71. C: Prokaryotes, or simple cells that lack a nucleus, appeared on Earth approximately 3.8 billion years ago. Eukaryotes, or complex cells, emerged 2 billion years ago, and arthropods developed about 570 million years ago. Amphibians emerged approximately 360 million years ago.

72. D: The Cambrian Explosion is best described as the dramatic increase in biodiversity that began about 530 million years ago and resulted in the emergence of complex animals over a period of millions of years. Evidence for this "explosion" of life comes mainly from fossil records. There are many possible explanations for it, ranging from an increase in oxygen levels to the development of eyes.

73. D: Expansion in the redshifts of galaxies, measurements of cosmic microwave background radiation, and measurements of the distribution of quasars and galaxies are all considered observational evidence in support of the Big Bang Theory. The abundance of certain "primordial elements" is also consistent with the theory.

74. C: The Cosmological Principle is best described as a working assumption that has testable structural consequences. The principle, which underlies existing cosmological theories, assumes that the view of the universe possessed by observers on Earth is not distorted by their observational location. The observable implications of this theory are homogeneity (the same types of observational evidence are available regardless of one's vantage point within the universe) and

isotropy (the same observational evidence is available by looking in any given direction from a single vantage point).

75. A: Redshift is observed when a light-emitting object moves away from an observer. The observation of cosmological redshift supports the notion that the universe is expanding and the distance between Earth and far away galaxies is increasing. Redshift is an increase in the wavelength of light that appears visually as a movement toward the "red" end of the spectrum.

76. D: The physical structure of the universe is thought to consist of filaments (walls of superclusters, clusters, and galaxies) that surround large, bubble-like voids. Filaments are the largest structures in the universe, with some forming huge structures like the Great Wall and the Sloan Great Wall.

77. B: It is true that galaxies are gravitationally bound so that structures within them orbit around the center. Galaxies do contain dark matter, and only the largest "giant" galaxies contain over one trillion stars. The smallest "dwarf" galaxies contain as few as 10 million stars. Clusters and superclusters are comprised of many galaxies.

78. A: The structure of the Milky Way galaxy is spiral, meaning it has curved "arms" stretching out from a central point. While spiral galaxies have a flat, disc-like appearance, elliptical galaxies are three-dimensional and appear to be roughly the same shape regardless of the viewing angle.

79. A: The Hertzsprung-Russell (H-R) Diagram is used primarily to determine a star's age by comparing its temperature and luminosity. These two variables are plotted, and a given star's values can be compared to those of other stars to estimate its age and evolutionary stage. Stars on the Main Sequence of the diagram have roughly proportional luminosity and temperature values, while white dwarf stars have low luminosity relative to their temperature. Some giant stars have low temperatures relative to their luminosity.

80. A: The distance from the Earth to the Sun is equal to one astronomical unit. An astronomical unit (AU) is equal to 93 million miles, and is far smaller than a light year or a parsec. A light year is defined as the distance light can travel in a vacuum in one year, and is equal to roughly 64,341 AU. A parsec is the parallax of one arcsecond, and is equal to 206.26×10^3 astronomical units.

81. B: The energy radiated by stars is produced by nuclear fusion. This is the process whereby the nuclei of individual atoms bind together to form heavier elements and release energy outward. By the time this energy, which is created in the star's core, reaches the outer walls of the star, it exists in the form of light.

82. A: The stream of charged particles that escape the Sun's gravitational pull is called solar wind. Solar wind is comprised primarily of protons and electrons, and

- 124 -

these particles are deflected away from the Earth by its magnetic field. When stray particles do manage to enter the atmosphere, they cause the aurorae (Northern and Southern Lights) and geomagnetic storms that can affect power grids.

83. C: Venus is not a gas giant. The four gas giants are Jupiter, Saturn, Uranus, and Neptune. While these "gas giants" are larger than Earth and are comprised mostly of gases, Venus is a terrestrial planet that is comparable in size to the Earth.

84. D: The asteroid belt in our solar system is located between Mars and Jupiter. The asteroid belt is populated by asteroids and dwarf planets that are distributed thinly enough that spacecraft can pass though the belt with relative ease.

85. D: Gravitational collapse and high-energy collisions are both proposed explanations for the formation of black holes. Gravitational collapse occurs when the outward pressure exerted by an object is too weak to resist that object's own gravity. Collisions that produce conditions of sufficient density could also, in theory, create black holes. The accretion of matter is considered observational evidence for the existence of black holes.

86. B: A total solar eclipse can be observed only by viewers located within the umbra. The umbra is the darkest part of the shadow, and the light source is not visible from it. The penumbra is the lighter portion of the shadow from which the light source is partially visible. In a solar eclipse, the Moon passes between the Earth and the Sun, and viewers in the umbra experience a total solar eclipse.

I. Basic Scientific Principles of Earth and Space Sciences

87. C: The atomic number of an element is defined by the total number of protons it contains, and elements are arranged on the periodic table by atomic number. The atomic mass of an element is the sum total of its protons and electrons.

88. B: The main distinction between the isotopes carbon-12 and carbon-13 is that they have different mass numbers. Isotopes of a given element all have the same atomic number, since atomic number (also known as proton number) is the defining characteristic of each element. However, they have different neutron numbers, which causes them to have varying mass numbers as well. Both carbon-12 and carbon-13 are stable isotopes, meaning they do not experience observable radioactive decay.

89. D: Electrons are elementary particles with no known components, so it is not true that they have a nucleus. Electrons are negatively charged, and they are arranged in levels. Electrons gravitate toward the lowest energy level possible, and they have very little mass (roughly 1/1836 of the mass of a proton).

90. A: Chemical compounds are formed when valence electrons from atoms of two different elements are shared or transferred. Valence electrons are the electrons

located in the outermost shell of the atom, and they occupy the highest energy level. Atoms may form compounds by sharing valence electrons (covalent bonding) or by transferring electrons.

91. C: The state of matter in which atoms have the strongest bond is the solid state. Matter, which is defined as any substance that has mass and occupies space, can exist as a solid, liquid, gas, or plasma. The atoms or molecules that form solids possess the strongest bonds, while those that form plasma possess the weakest bonds.

92. B: A closed thermodynamic system can exchange heat and work, but not matter, with its surrounding environment. In contrast, an isolated system cannot exchange heat, work, or matter with its surrounding environment, so its mass and energy levels always remain constant. Open systems can exchange heat, work, and mass with their surrounding environments.

93. A: The formula for calculating kinetic energy is $\frac{1}{2}mv^2$, where m=mass and v=velocity. Kinetic energy is defined as the energy of an object in motion. Potential energy, or stored energy, is measured using the formula mgh, where m=mass, g=gravity, and h=height.

94. B: The first law of classical thermodynamics states that energy can neither be created nor destroyed. The zeroth law is concerned with thermodynamic equilibrium, and the second and third laws discuss entropy.

95. C: James Hutton is best known for proposing the theory of uniformitarianism. This geological theory, which is essentially the opposite of catastrophism, suggests that the laws and forces acting on the Earth have remained basically the same since the beginning of geologic time.

96. A: The correct formula for converting Fahrenheit measurements to Celsius measurements is 5/9 (F – 32), where F is the temperature in Fahrenheit.

97. A: A calorimeter is used to measure changes in heat. This instrument uses a thermometer to measure the amount of energy necessary to increase the temperature of water.

98. A: Commercial nuclear reactors generate electricity through the process of nuclear fission. The fission process is used to heat water, which in turn generates steam that is used to produce electricity. This process is controlled to ensure safety, but it does produce nuclear waste that requires the use of extensive procedures to dispose of it safely.

99. C: The results of the regression analysis show that there is a weak positive correlation between the two variables, as evidenced by the fact that data points with higher values for the independent variable (x-axis) also have higher corresponding

values for the dependent variable (y-axis). However, correlation does not equal causation, and it cannot be established that a change in the independent variable causes a corresponding change in the dependent variable without additional information.

100. B: Random error could be caused by extraneous disturbances that cannot be controlled. Random error is that which does not affect experimental results in a consistent, patterned way. In contrast, systematic error affects all experimental results consistently. For example, if an instrument is calibrated improperly, all experimental results will be skewed in the same direction.

Secret Key #1 - Time is Your Greatest Enemy

Pace Yourself

Wear a watch. At the beginning of the test, check the time (or start a chronometer on your watch to count the minutes), and check the time after every few questions to make sure you are "on schedule."

If you are forced to speed up, do it efficiently. Usually one or more answer choices can be eliminated without too much difficulty. Above all, don't panic. Don't speed up and just begin guessing at random choices. By pacing yourself, and continually monitoring your progress against your watch, you will always know exactly how far ahead or behind you are with your available time. If you find that you are one minute behind on the test, don't skip one question without spending any time on it, just to catch back up. Take 15 fewer seconds on the next four questions, and after four questions you'll have caught back up. Once you catch back up, you can continue working each problem at your normal pace.

Furthermore, don't dwell on the problems that you were rushed on. If a problem was taking up too much time and you made a hurried guess, it must be difficult. The difficult questions are the ones you are most likely to miss anyway, so it isn't a big loss. It is better to end with more time than you need than to run out of time.

Lastly, sometimes it is beneficial to slow down if you are constantly getting ahead of time. You are always more likely to catch a careless mistake by working more slowly than quickly, and among very high-scoring test takers (those who are likely to have lots of time left over), careless errors affect the score more than mastery of material.

Secret Key #2 - Guessing is not Guesswork

You probably know that guessing is a good idea. Unlike other standardized tests, there is no penalty for getting a wrong answer. Even if you have no idea about a question, you still have a 20-25% chance of getting it right.

Most test takers do not understand the impact that proper guessing can have on their score. Unless you score extremely high, guessing will significantly contribute to your final score.

Monkeys Take the Test

What most test takers don't realize is that to insure that 20-25% chance, you have to guess randomly. If you put 20 monkeys in a room to take this test, assuming they answered once per question and behaved themselves, on average they would get 20-25% of the questions correct. Put 20 test takers in the room, and the average will be much lower among guessed questions. Why?

1. The test writers intentionally write deceptive answer choices that "look" right. A test taker has no idea about a question, so he picks the "best looking" answer, which is often wrong. The monkey has no idea what looks good and what doesn't, so it will consistently be right about 20-25% of the time.
2. Test takers will eliminate answer choices from the guessing pool based on a hunch or intuition. Simple but correct answers often get excluded, leaving a 0% chance of being correct. The monkey has no clue, and often gets lucky with the best choice.

This is why the process of elimination endorsed by most test courses is flawed and detrimental to your performance. Test takers don't guess; they make an ignorant stab in the dark that is usually worse than random.

$5 Challenge

Let me introduce one of the most valuable ideas of this course—the $5 challenge:

- *You only mark your "best guess" if you are willing to bet $5 on it.*
- *You only eliminate choices from guessing if you are willing to bet $5 on it.*

Why $5? Five dollars is an amount of money that is small yet not insignificant, and can really add up fast (20 questions could cost you $100). Likewise, each answer choice on one question of the test will have a small impact on your overall score, but it can really add up to a lot of points in the end.

The process of elimination IS valuable. The following shows your chance of guessing it right:

If you eliminate wrong answer choices until only this many remain:	Chance of getting it correct:
1	100%
2	50%
3	33%

However, if you accidentally eliminate the right answer or go on a hunch for an incorrect answer, your chances drop dramatically—to 0%. By guessing among all the answer choices, you are GUARANTEED to have a shot at the right answer.

That's why the $5 test is so valuable. If you give up the advantage and safety of a pure guess, it had better be worth the risk.

What we still haven't covered is how to be sure that whatever guess you make is truly random. Here's the easiest way:

- *Always pick the first answer choice among those remaining.*

Such a technique means that you have decided, **before you see a single test question**, exactly how you are going to guess, and since the order of choices tells you nothing about which one is correct, this guessing technique is perfectly random.

This section is not meant to scare you away from making educated guesses or eliminating choices; you just need to define when a choice is worth eliminating. The $5 test, along with a pre-defined random guessing strategy, is the best way to make sure you reap all of the benefits of guessing.

Secret Key #3 - Practice Smarter, Not Harder

Many test takers delay the test preparation process because they dread the awful amounts of practice time they think necessary to succeed on the test. We have refined an effective method that will take you only a fraction of the time.

There are a number of "obstacles" in the path to success. Among these are answering questions, finishing in time, and mastering test-taking strategies. All must be executed on the day of the test at peak performance, or your score will suffer. The test is a mental marathon that has a large impact on your future.

Just like a marathon runner, it is important to work your way up to the full challenge. So first you just worry about questions, and then time, and finally strategy:

Success Strategy

1. Find a good source for practice tests.
2. If you are willing to make a larger time investment, consider using more than one study guide. Often the different approaches of multiple authors will help you "get" difficult concepts.
3. Take a practice test with no time constraints, with all study helps, "open book." Take your time with questions and focus on applying strategies.
4. Take a practice test with time constraints, with all guides, "open book."
5. Take a final practice test without open material and with time limits.

If you have time to take more practice tests, just repeat step 5. By gradually exposing yourself to the full rigors of the test environment, you will condition your mind to the stress of test day and maximize your success.

Secret Key #4 - Prepare, Don't Procrastinate

Let me state an obvious fact: if you take the test three times, you will probably get three different scores. This is due to the way you feel on test day, the level of preparedness you have, and the version of the test you see. Despite the test writers' claims to the contrary, some versions of the test WILL be easier for you than others.

Since your future depends so much on your score, you should maximize your chances of success. In order to maximize the likelihood of success, you've got to prepare in advance. This means taking practice tests and spending time learning the information and test taking strategies you will need to succeed.

Never go take the actual test as a "practice" test, expecting that you can just take it again if you need to. Take all the practice tests you can on your own, but when you go to take the official test, be prepared, be focused, and do your best the first time!

Secret Key #5 - Test Yourself

Everyone knows that time is money. There is no need to spend too much of your time or too little of your time preparing for the test. You should only spend as much of your precious time preparing as is necessary for you to get the score you need.

Once you have taken a practice test under real conditions of time constraints, then you will know if you are ready for the test or not.

If you have scored extremely high the first time that you take the practice test, then there is not much point in spending countless hours studying. You are already there.

Benchmark your abilities by retaking practice tests and seeing how much you have improved. Once you consistently score high enough to guarantee success, then you are ready.

If you have scored well below where you need, then knuckle down and begin studying in earnest. Check your improvement regularly through the use of practice tests under real conditions. Above all, don't worry, panic, or give up. The key is perseverance!

Then, when you go to take the test, remain confident and remember how well you did on the practice tests. If you can score high enough on a practice test, then you can do the same on the real thing.

General Strategies

The most important thing you can do is to ignore your fears and jump into the test immediately. Do not be overwhelmed by any strange-sounding terms. You have to jump into the test like jumping into a pool—all at once is the easiest way.

Make Predictions

As you read and understand the question, try to guess what the answer will be. Remember that several of the answer choices are wrong, and once you begin reading them, your mind will immediately become cluttered with answer choices designed to throw you off. Your mind is typically the most focused immediately after you have read the question and digested its contents. If you can, try to predict what the correct answer will be. You may be surprised at what you can predict.

Quickly scan the choices and see if your prediction is in the listed answer choices. If it is, then you can be quite confident that you have the right answer. It still won't hurt to check the other answer choices, but most of the time, you've got it!

Answer the Question

It may seem obvious to only pick answer choices that answer the question, but the test writers can create some excellent answer choices that are wrong. Don't pick an answer just because it sounds right, or you believe it to be true. It MUST answer the question. Once you've made your selection, always go back and check it against the question and make sure that you didn't misread the question and that the answer choice does answer the question posed.

Benchmark

After you read the first answer choice, decide if you think it sounds correct or not. If it doesn't, move on to the next answer choice. If it does, mentally mark that answer choice. This doesn't mean that you've definitely selected it as your answer choice, it just means that it's the best you've seen thus far. Go ahead and read the next choice. If the next choice is worse than the one you've already selected, keep going to the next answer choice. If the next choice is better than the choice you've already selected, mentally mark the new answer choice as your best guess.

The first answer choice that you select becomes your standard. Every other answer choice must be benchmarked against that standard. That choice is correct until proven otherwise by another answer choice beating it out. Once you've decided that no other answer choice seems as good, do one final check to ensure that your answer choice answers the question posed.

Valid Information

Don't discount any of the information provided in the question. Every piece of information may be necessary to determine the correct answer. None of the information in the question is there to throw you off (while the answer choices will certainly have information to throw you off). If two seemingly unrelated topics are discussed, don't ignore either. You can be confident there is a relationship, or it wouldn't be included in the question, and you are probably going to have to determine what is that relationship to find the answer.

Avoid "Fact Traps"

Don't get distracted by a choice that is factually true. Your search is for the answer that answers the question. Stay focused and don't fall for an answer that is true but irrelevant. Always go back to the question and make sure you're choosing an answer that actually answers the question and is not just a true statement. An answer can be factually correct, but it MUST answer the question asked. Additionally, two answers can both be seemingly correct, so be sure to read all of the answer choices, and make sure that you get the one that BEST answers the question.

Milk the Question

Some of the questions may throw you completely off. They might deal with a subject you have not been exposed to, or one that you haven't reviewed in years. While your lack of knowledge about the subject will be a hindrance, the question itself can give you many clues that will help you find the correct answer. Read the question carefully and look for clues. Watch particularly for adjectives and nouns describing difficult terms or words that you don't recognize. Regardless of whether you completely understand a word or not, replacing it with a synonym, either provided or one you more familiar with, may help you to understand what the questions are asking. Rather than wracking your mind about specific detailed information concerning a difficult term or word, try to use mental substitutes that are easier to understand.

The Trap of Familiarity

Don't just choose a word because you recognize it. On difficult questions, you may not recognize a number of words in the answer choices. The test writers don't put "make-believe" words on the test, so don't think that just because you only recognize all the words in one answer choice that that answer choice must be correct. If you only recognize words in one answer choice, then focus on that one. Is it correct? Try your best to determine if it is correct. If it is, that's great. If not, eliminate it. Each word and answer choice you eliminate increases your chances of getting the question correct, even if you then have to guess among the unfamiliar choices.

Eliminate Answers

Eliminate choices as soon as you realize they are wrong. But be careful! Make sure you consider all of the possible answer choices. Just because one appears right, doesn't mean that the next one won't be even better! The test writers will usually put more than one good answer choice for every question, so read all of them. Don't worry if you are stuck between two that seem right. By getting down to just two remaining possible choices, your odds are now 50/50. Rather than wasting too much time, play the odds. You are guessing, but guessing wisely because you've been able to knock out some of the answer choices that you know are wrong. If you are eliminating choices and realize that the last answer choice you are left with is also obviously wrong, don't panic. Start over and consider each choice again. There may easily be something that you missed the first time and will realize on the second pass.

Tough Questions

If you are stumped on a problem or it appears too hard or too difficult, don't waste time. Move on! Remember though, if you can quickly check for obviously incorrect answer choices, your chances of guessing correctly are greatly improved. Before you completely give up, at least try to knock out a couple of possible answers. Eliminate what you can and then guess at the remaining answer choices before moving on.

Brainstorm

If you get stuck on a difficult question, spend a few seconds quickly brainstorming. Run through the complete list of possible answer choices. Look at each choice and ask yourself, "Could this answer the question satisfactorily?" Go through each answer choice and consider it independently of the others. By systematically going through all possibilities, you may find something that you would otherwise overlook. Remember though that when you get stuck, it's important to try to keep moving.

Read Carefully

Understand the problem. Read the question and answer choices carefully. Don't miss the question because you misread the terms. You have plenty of time to read each question thoroughly and make sure you understand what is being asked. Yet a happy medium must be attained, so don't waste too much time. You must read carefully, but efficiently.

Face Value

When in doubt, use common sense. Always accept the situation in the problem at face value. Don't read too much into it. These problems will not require you to make huge leaps of logic. The test writers aren't trying to throw you off with a cheap trick. If you have to go beyond creativity and make a leap of logic in order to have an answer choice answer the question, then you should look at the other answer choices. Don't overcomplicate the problem by creating theoretical relationships or explanations that will warp time or space. These are normal problems rooted in reality. It's just that the applicable relationship or explanation may not be readily apparent and you have to figure things out. Use your common sense to interpret anything that isn't clear.

Prefixes

If you're having trouble with a word in the question or answer choices, try dissecting it. Take advantage of every clue that the word might include. Prefixes

Dear Friend,

Thank you for ordering Mometrix products!

We take very seriously that you are entrusting your test preparation needs to us. We have meticulously prepared these materials to ensure we are offering you the most concise, relevant study aid possible. There are many resources available for your exam and we sincerely appreciate you choosing ours to help you attain the highest score within your ability to achieve.

You are about to experience an incredible transformation. Over the next few hours, days, weeks, or months of studying, you will transition from your current level of preparedness to an understanding of the exam content you never thought possible. You now hold in your hands the information you most need to know in order to succeed on your exam. Regardless of whether this is your first time to take the exam or your fifth time, our goal is to give you exactly what you need to maximize your score so you can go where you most want to go and be what you most want to be.

In addition to the products you have ordered from us, we have included a few bonuses that will help in your preparation. Be on the lookout for a special bonus website included in each product that offers additional tips and insights. In response to the test anxiety many people experience, we have also developed a free report to help you overcome this obstacle that you can access by visiting: www.mometrix.com/testanxiety.

From the many families here at Mometrix to yours, we sincerely thank you and wish you the best on your exam and every journey life has in store for you.

If you have any questions or suggestions as to how we can improve our products or service, please contact us at 800-673-8175 or support@mometrix.com.

Sincerely,

Jay Willis
Vice President of Sales
Mometrix Test Preparation

P.S. - We would greatly appreciate you recommending our products to your friends and colleagues!

and suffixes can be a huge help. Usually they allow you to determine a basic meaning. Pre- means before, post- means after, pro - is positive, de- is negative. From these prefixes and suffixes, you can get an idea of the general meaning of the word and try to put it into context. Beware though of any traps. Just because con- is the opposite of pro-, doesn't necessarily mean congress is the opposite of progress!

Hedge Phrases

Watch out for critical hedge phrases, led off with words such as "likely," "may," "can," "sometimes," "often," "almost," "mostly," "usually," "generally," "rarely," and "sometimes." Question writers insert these hedge phrases to cover every possibility. Often an answer choice will be wrong simply because it leaves no room for exception. Unless the situation calls for them, avoid answer choices that have definitive words like "exactly," and "always."

Switchback Words

Stay alert for "switchbacks." These are the words and phrases frequently used to alert you to shifts in thought. The most common switchback word is "but." Others include "although," "however," "nevertheless," "on the other hand," "even though," "while," "in spite of," "despite," and "regardless of."

New Information

Correct answer choices will rarely have completely new information included. Answer choices typically are straightforward reflections of the material asked about and will directly relate to the question. If a new piece of information is included in an answer choice that doesn't even seem to relate to the topic being asked about, then that answer choice is likely incorrect. All of the information needed to answer the question is usually provided for you in the question. You should not have to make guesses that are unsupported or choose answer choices that require unknown information that cannot be reasoned from what is given.

Time Management

On technical questions, don't get lost on the technical terms. Don't spend too much time on any one question. If you don't know what a term means, then odds are you aren't going to get much further since you don't have a dictionary. You should be able to immediately recognize whether or not you know a term. If you don't, work with the other clues that you have—the other answer choices and terms provided— but don't waste too much time trying to figure out a difficult term that you don't know.

Contextual Clues

Look for contextual clues. An answer can be right but not the correct answer. The contextual clues will help you find the answer that is most right and is correct. Understand the context in which a phrase or statement is made. This will help you make important distinctions.

- 137 -

Don't Panic

Panicking will not answer any questions for you; therefore, it isn't helpful. When you first see the question, if your mind goes blank, take a deep breath. Force yourself to mechanically go through the steps of solving the problem using the strategies you've learned.

Pace Yourself

Don't get clock fever. It's easy to be overwhelmed when you're looking at a page full of questions, your mind is full of random thoughts and feeling confused, and the clock is ticking down faster than you would like. Calm down and maintain the pace that you have set for yourself. As long as you are on track by monitoring your pace, you are guaranteed to have enough time for yourself. When you get to the last few minutes of the test, it may seem like you won't have enough time left, but if you only have as many questions as you should have left at that point, then you're right on track!

Answer Selection

The best way to pick an answer choice is to eliminate all of those that are wrong, until only one is left and confirm that is the correct answer. Sometimes though, an answer choice may immediately look right. Be careful! Take a second to make sure that the other choices are not equally obvious. Don't make a hasty mistake. There are only two times that you should stop before checking other answers. First is when you are positive that the answer choice you have selected is correct. Second is when time is almost out and you have to make a quick guess!

Check Your Work

Since you will probably not know every term listed and the answer to every question, it is important that you get credit for the ones that you do know. Don't miss any questions through careless mistakes. If at all possible, try to take a second to look back over your answer selection and make sure you've selected the correct answer choice and haven't made a costly careless mistake (such as marking an answer choice that you didn't mean to mark). The time it takes for this quick double check should more than pay for itself in caught mistakes.

Beware of Directly Quoted Answers

Sometimes an answer choice will repeat word for word a portion of the question or reference section. However, beware of such exact duplication. It may be a trap! More than likely, the correct choice will paraphrase or summarize a point, rather than being exactly the same wording.

Slang

Scientific sounding answers are better than slang ones. An answer choice that begins "To compare the outcomes…" is much more likely to be correct than one that begins "Because some people insisted…"

Extreme Statements

Avoid wild answers that throw out highly controversial ideas that are proclaimed as established fact. An answer choice that states the "process should used in certain situations, if…" is much more likely to be correct than one that states the "process should be discontinued completely." The first is a calm rational statement and doesn't even make a definitive, uncompromising stance, using a hedge word "if" to provide wiggle room, whereas the second choice is a radical idea and far more extreme.

Answer Choice Families

When you have two or more answer choices that are direct opposites or parallels, one of them is usually the correct answer. For instance, if one answer choice states "x increases" and another answer choice states "x decreases" or "y increases," then those two or three answer choices are very similar in construction and fall into the same family of answer choices. A family of answer choices consists of two or three answer choices, very similar in construction, but often with directly opposite meanings. Usually the correct answer choice will be in that family of answer choices. The "odd man out" or answer choice that doesn't seem to fit the parallel construction of the other answer choices is more likely to be incorrect.

Special Report: How to Overcome Test Anxiety

The very nature of tests caters to some level of anxiety, nervousness, or tension, just as we feel for any important event that occurs in our lives. A little bit of anxiety or nervousness can be a good thing. It helps us with motivation, and makes achievement just that much sweeter. However, too much anxiety can be a problem, especially if it hinders our ability to function and perform.

"Test anxiety," is the term that refers to the emotional reactions that some test-takers experience when faced with a test or exam. Having a fear of testing and exams is based upon a rational fear, since the test-taker's performance can shape the course of an academic career. Nevertheless, experiencing excessive fear of examinations will only interfere with the test-taker's ability to perform and chance to be successful.

There are a large variety of causes that can contribute to the development and sensation of test anxiety. These include, but are not limited to, lack of preparation and worrying about issues surrounding the test.

Lack of Preparation

Lack of preparation can be identified by the following behaviors or situations:
- Not scheduling enough time to study, and therefore cramming the night before the test or exam
- Managing time poorly, to create the sensation that there is not enough time to do everything
- Failing to organize the text information in advance, so that the study material consists of the entire text and not simply the pertinent information
- Poor overall studying habits

Worrying, on the other hand, can be related to both the test taker, or many other factors around him/her that will be affected by the results of the test. These include worrying about:
- Previous performances on similar exams, or exams in general
- How friends and other students are achieving
- The negative consequences that will result from a poor grade or failure

There are three primary elements to test anxiety. Physical components, which involve the same typical bodily reactions as those to acute anxiety (to be discussed below). Emotional factors have to do with fear or panic. Mental or cognitive issues concerning attention spans and memory abilities.

Physical Signals

There are many different symptoms of test anxiety, and these are not limited to mental and emotional strain. Frequently there are a range of physical signals that will let a test taker know that he/she is suffering from test anxiety. These bodily changes can include the following:

- Perspiring
- Sweaty palms
- Wet, trembling hands
- Nausea
- Dry mouth
- A knot in the stomach
- Headache
- Faintness
- Muscle tension
- Aching shoulders, back and neck
- Rapid heart beat
- Feeling too hot/cold

To recognize the sensation of test anxiety, a test-taker should monitor him/herself for the following sensations:

- The physical distress symptoms as listed above
- Emotional sensitivity, expressing emotional feelings such as the need to cry or laugh too much, or a sensation of anger or helplessness
- A decreased ability to think, causing the test-taker to blank out or have racing thoughts that are hard to organize or control.

Though most students will feel some level of anxiety when faced with a test or exam, the majority can cope with that anxiety and maintain it at a manageable level. However, those who cannot are faced with a very real and very serious condition, which can and should be controlled for the immeasurable benefit of this sufferer.

Naturally, these sensations lead to negative results for the testing experience. The most common effects of test anxiety have to do with nervousness and mental blocking.

Nervousness

Nervousness can appear in several different levels:

- The test-taker's difficulty, or even inability to read and understand the questions on the test
- The difficulty or inability to organize thoughts to a coherent form

- The difficulty or inability to recall key words and concepts relating to the testing questions (especially essays)
- The receipt of poor grades on a test, though the test material was well known by the test taker

Conversely, a person may also experience mental blocking, which involves:
- Blanking out on test questions
- Only remembering the correct answers to the questions when the test has already finished.

Fortunately for test anxiety sufferers, beating these feelings, to a large degree, has to do with proper preparation. When a test taker has a feeling of preparedness, then anxiety will be dramatically lessened.

The first step to resolving anxiety issues is to distinguish which of the two types of anxiety are being suffered. If the anxiety is a direct result of a lack of preparation, this should be considered a normal reaction, and the anxiety level (as opposed to the test results) shouldn't be anything to worry about. However, if, when adequately prepared, the test-taker still panics, blanks out, or seems to overreact, this is not a fully rational reaction. While this can be considered normal too, there are many ways to combat and overcome these effects.

Remember that anxiety cannot be entirely eliminated, however, there are ways to minimize it, to make the anxiety easier to manage. Preparation is one of the best ways to minimize test anxiety. Therefore the following techniques are wise in order to best fight off any anxiety that may want to build.

To begin with, try to avoid cramming before a test, whenever it is possible. By trying to memorize an entire term's worth of information in one day, you'll be shocking your system, and not giving yourself a very good chance to absorb the information. This is an easy path to anxiety, so for those who suffer from test anxiety, cramming should not even be considered an option.

Instead of cramming, work throughout the semester to combine all of the material which is presented throughout the semester, and work on it gradually as the course goes by, making sure to master the main concepts first, leaving minor details for a week or so before the test.

To study for the upcoming exam, be sure to pose questions that may be on the examination, to gauge the ability to answer them by integrating the ideas from your texts, notes and lectures, as well as any supplementary readings.
If it is truly impossible to cover all of the information that was covered in that particular term, concentrate on the most important portions, that can be covered very well. Learn these concepts as best as possible, so that when the test comes, a goal can be made to use these concepts as presentations of your knowledge.

In addition to study habits, changes in attitude are critical to beating a struggle with test anxiety. In fact, an improvement of the perspective over the entire test-taking experience can actually help a test taker to enjoy studying and therefore improve the overall experience. Be certain not to overemphasize the significance of the grade - know that the result of the test is neither a reflection of self worth, nor is it a measure of intelligence; one grade will not predict a person's future success.

To improve an overall testing outlook, the following steps should be tried:
- Keeping in mind that the most reasonable expectation for taking a test is to expect to try to demonstrate as much of what you know as you possibly can.
- Reminding ourselves that a test is only one test; this is not the only one, and there will be others.
- The thought of thinking of oneself in an irrational, all-or-nothing term should be avoided at all costs.
- A reward should be designated for after the test, so there's something to look forward to. Whether it be going to a movie, going out to eat, or simply visiting friends, schedule it in advance, and do it no matter what result is expected on the exam.

Test-takers should also keep in mind that the basics are some of the most important things, even beyond anti-anxiety techniques and studying. Never neglect the basic social, emotional and biological needs, in order to try to absorb information. In order to best achieve, these three factors must be held as just as important as the studying itself.

Study Steps

Remember the following important steps for studying:
- Maintain healthy nutrition and exercise habits. Continue both your recreational activities and social pass times. These both contribute to your physical and emotional well being.
- Be certain to get a good amount of sleep, especially the night before the test, because when you're overtired you are not able to perform to the best of your best ability.
- Keep the studying pace to a moderate level by taking breaks when they are needed, and varying the work whenever possible, to keep the mind fresh instead of getting bored.
- When enough studying has been done that all the material that can be learned has been learned, and the test taker is prepared for the test, stop studying and do something relaxing such as listening to music, watching a movie, or taking a warm bubble bath.

There are also many other techniques to minimize the uneasiness or apprehension that is experienced along with test anxiety before, during, or even after the examination. In fact, there are a great deal of things that can be done to stop anxiety from interfering with lifestyle and performance. Again, remember that anxiety will not be eliminated entirely, and it shouldn't be. Otherwise that "up" feeling for exams would not exist, and most of us depend on that sensation to perform better than usual. However, this anxiety has to be at a level that is manageable.

Of course, as we have just discussed, being prepared for the exam is half the battle right away. Attending all classes, finding out what knowledge will be expected on the exam, and knowing the exam schedules are easy steps to lowering anxiety. Keeping up with work will remove the need to cram, and efficient study habits will eliminate wasted time. Studying should be done in an ideal location for concentration, so that it is simple to become interested in the material and give it complete attention. A method such as SQ3R (Survey, Question, Read, Recite, Review) is a wonderful key to follow to make sure that the study habits are as effective as possible, especially in the case of learning from a textbook. Flashcards are great techniques for memorization. Learning to take good notes will mean that notes will be full of useful information, so that less sifting will need to be done to seek out what is pertinent for studying. Reviewing notes after class and then again on occasion will keep the information fresh in the mind. From notes that have been taken summary sheets and outlines can be made for simpler reviewing.

A study group can also be a very motivational and helpful place to study, as there will be a sharing of ideas, all of the minds can work together, to make sure that everyone understands, and the studying will be made more interesting because it will be a social occasion.

Basically, though, as long as the test-taker remains organized and self confident, with efficient study habits, less time will need to be spent studying, and higher grades will be achieved.

To become self confident, there are many useful steps. The first of these is "self talk." It has been shown through extensive research, that self-talk for students who suffer from test anxiety, should be well monitored, in order to make sure that it contributes to self confidence as opposed to sinking the student. Frequently the self talk of test-anxious students is negative or self-defeating, thinking that everyone else is smarter and faster, that they always mess up, and that if they don't do well, they'll fail the entire course. It is important to decreasing anxiety that awareness is made of self talk. Try writing any negative self thoughts and then disputing them with a positive statement instead. Begin self-encouragement as though it was a friend speaking. Repeat positive statements to help reprogram the mind to believing in successes instead of failures.

Helpful Techniques

Other extremely helpful techniques include:
- Self-visualization of doing well and reaching goals
- While aiming for an "A" level of understanding, don't try to "overprotect" by setting your expectations lower. This will only convince the mind to stop studying in order to meet the lower expectations.
- Don't make comparisons with the results or habits of other students. These are individual factors, and different things work for different people, causing different results.
- Strive to become an expert in learning what works well, and what can be done in order to improve. Consider collecting this data in a journal.
- Create rewards for after studying instead of doing things before studying that will only turn into avoidance behaviors.
- Make a practice of relaxing - by using methods such as progressive relaxation, self-hypnosis, guided imagery, etc - in order to make relaxation an automatic sensation.
- Work on creating a state of relaxed concentration so that concentrating will take on the focus of the mind, so that none will be wasted on worrying.
- Take good care of the physical self by eating well and getting enough sleep.
- Plan in time for exercise and stick to this plan.

Beyond these techniques, there are other methods to be used before, during and after the test that will help the test-taker perform well in addition to overcoming anxiety.

Before the exam comes the academic preparation. This involves establishing a study schedule and beginning at least one week before the actual date of the test. By doing this, the anxiety of not having enough time to study for the test will be automatically eliminated. Moreover, this will make the studying a much more effective experience, ensuring that the learning will be an easier process. This relieves much undue pressure on the test-taker.

Summary sheets, note cards, and flash cards with the main concepts and examples of these main concepts should be prepared in advance of the actual studying time. A topic should never be eliminated from this process. By omitting a topic because it isn't expected to be on the test is only setting up the test-taker for anxiety should it actually appear on the exam. Utilize the course syllabus for laying out the topics that should be studied. Carefully go over the notes that were made in class, paying special attention to any of the issues that the professor took special care to emphasize while lecturing in class. In the textbooks, use the chapter review, or if possible, the chapter tests, to begin your review.

It may even be possible to ask the instructor what information will be covered on the exam, or what the format of the exam will be (for example, multiple choice, essay, free form, true-false). Additionally, see if it is possible to find out how many questions will be on the test. If a review sheet or sample test has been offered by the professor, make good use of it, above anything else, for the preparation for the test. Another great resource for getting to know the examination is reviewing tests from previous semesters. Use these tests to review, and aim to achieve a 100% score on each of the possible topics. With a few exceptions, the goal that you set for yourself is the highest one that you will reach.

Take all of the questions that were assigned as homework, and rework them to any other possible course material. The more problems reworked, the more skill and confidence will form as a result. When forming the solution to a problem, write out each of the steps. Don't simply do head work. By doing as many steps on paper as possible, much clarification and therefore confidence will be formed. Do this with as many homework problems as possible, before checking the answers. By checking the answer after each problem, a reinforcement will exist, that will not be on the exam. Study situations should be as exam-like as possible, to prime the test-taker's system for the experience. By waiting to check the answers at the end, a psychological advantage will be formed, to decrease the stress factor.

Another fantastic reason for not cramming is the avoidance of confusion in concepts, especially when it comes to mathematics. 8-10 hours of study will become one hundred percent more effective if it is spread out over a week or at least several days, instead of doing it all in one sitting. Recognize that the human brain requires time in order to assimilate new material, so frequent breaks and a span of study time over several days will be much more beneficial.

Additionally, don't study right up until the point of the exam. Studying should stop a minimum of one hour before the exam begins. This allows the brain to rest and put things in their proper order. This will also provide the time to become as relaxed as possible when going into the examination room. The test-taker will also have time to eat well and eat sensibly. Know that the brain needs food as much as the rest of the body. With enough food and enough sleep, as well as a relaxed attitude, the body and the mind are primed for success.

Avoid any anxious classmates who are talking about the exam. These students only spread anxiety, and are not worth sharing the anxious sentimentalities.

Before the test also involves creating a positive attitude, so mental preparation should also be a point of concentration. There are many keys to creating a positive attitude. Should fears become rushing in, make a visualization of taking the exam, doing well, and seeing an A written on the paper. Write out a list of affirmations that will bring a feeling of confidence, such as "I am doing well in my English class," "I studied well and know my material," "I enjoy this class." Even if the affirmations aren't believed at first, it sends a positive message to the subconscious which will result in an alteration of the overall belief system, which is the system that creates reality.

If a sensation of panic begins, work with the fear and imagine the very worst! Work through the entire scenario of not passing the test, failing the entire course, and dropping out of school, followed by not getting a job, and pushing a shopping cart through the dark alley where you'll live. This will place things into perspective! Then, practice deep breathing and create a visualization of the opposite situation - achieving an "A" on the exam, passing the entire course, receiving the degree at a graduation ceremony.

On the day of the test, there are many things to be done to ensure the best results, as well as the most calm outlook. The following stages are suggested in order to maximize test-taking potential:

- Begin the examination day with a moderate breakfast, and avoid any coffee or beverages with caffeine if the test taker is prone to jitters. Even people who are used to managing caffeine can feel jittery or light-headed when it is taken on a test day.
- Attempt to do something that is relaxing before the examination begins. As last minute cramming clouds the mastering of overall concepts, it is better to use this time to create a calming outlook.
- Be certain to arrive at the test location well in advance, in order to provide time to select a location that is away from doors, windows and other distractions, as well as giving enough time to relax before the test begins.
- Keep away from anxiety generating classmates who will upset the sensation of stability and relaxation that is being attempted before the exam.
- Should the waiting period before the exam begins cause anxiety, create a self-distraction by reading a light magazine or something else that is relaxing and simple.

During the exam itself, read the entire exam from beginning to end, and find out how much time should be allotted to each individual problem. Once writing the exam, should more time be taken for a problem, it should be abandoned, in order to begin another problem. If there is time at the end, the unfinished problem can always be returned to and completed.

Read the instructions very carefully - twice - so that unpleasant surprises won't follow during or after the exam has ended.

When writing the exam, pretend that the situation is actually simply the completion of homework within a library, or at home. This will assist in forming a relaxed atmosphere, and will allow the brain extra focus for the complex thinking function.

Begin the exam with all of the questions with which the most confidence is felt. This will build the confidence level regarding the entire exam and will begin a quality momentum. This will also create encouragement for trying the problems where uncertainty resides.

Going with the "gut instinct" is always the way to go when solving a problem. Second guessing should be avoided at all costs. Have confidence in the ability to do well.

For essay questions, create an outline in advance that will keep the mind organized and make certain that all of the points are remembered. For multiple choice, read every answer, even if the correct one has been spotted - a better one may exist.

Continue at a pace that is reasonable and not rushed, in order to be able to work carefully. Provide enough time to go over the answers at the end, to check for small errors that can be corrected.

Should a feeling of panic begin, breathe deeply, and think of the feeling of the body releasing sand through its pores. Visualize a calm, peaceful place, and include all of the sights, sounds and sensations of this image. Continue the deep breathing, and take a few minutes to continue this with closed eyes. When all is well again, return to the test.

If a "blanking" occurs for a certain question, skip it and move on to the next question. There will be time to return to the other question later. Get everything done that can be done, first, to guarantee all the grades that can be compiled, and to build all of the confidence possible. Then return to the weaker questions to build the marks from there.

Remember, one's own reality can be created, so as long as the belief is there, success will follow. And remember: anxiety can happen later, right now, there's an exam to be written!

After the examination is complete, whether there is a feeling for a good grade or a bad grade, don't dwell on the exam, and be certain to follow through on the reward that was promised...and enjoy it! Don't dwell on any mistakes that have been made, as there is nothing that can be done at this point anyway.

Additionally, don't begin to study for the next test right away. Do something relaxing for a while, and let the mind relax and prepare itself to begin absorbing information again.

From the results of the exam - both the grade and the entire experience, be certain to learn from what has gone on. Perfect studying habits and work some more on confidence in order to make the next examination experience even better than the last one.

Learn to avoid places where openings occurred for laziness, procrastination and day dreaming.

Use the time between this exam and the next one to better learn to relax, even learning to relax on cue, so that any anxiety can be controlled during the next exam. Learn how to relax the body. Slouch in your chair if that helps. Tighten and then relax all of the different muscle groups, one group at a time, beginning with the feet and then working all the way up to the neck and face. This will ultimately relax the muscles more than they were to begin with. Learn how to breathe deeply and comfortably, and focus on this breathing going in and out as a relaxing thought. With every exhale, repeat the word "relax."

As common as test anxiety is, it is very possible to overcome it. Make yourself one of the test-takers who overcome this frustrating hindrance.

Additional Bonus Material

Due to our efforts to try to keep this book to a manageable length, we've created a link that will give you access to all of your additional bonus material.

Please visit http://www.mometrix.com/bonus948/csetearthplsci to access the information.